The Essential Guide to Creative Textiles

Edited by Sue Richardson
Published by Word4Word

Front Cover Images

Clockwise from top left

Pleated textiles by Jo Buckler at C2+ Textile Gallery, see Art Galleries and Exhibitions, p. 14

'Interplay' by Alicia Merrett, see Textile Artists and Designers, p. 103

Two students enjoying a batik holiday course on the Lancaster University summer programme, see Summer Schools, p. 89

'Off the Straight and Narrow', Annette Claxton, see Textile Artists and Designers, p. 96

'Siliqua 1, 2 and 3', Emma Reynolds (photo by Tony Millings), see Textile Artists and Designers, p. 104

'Queen of Diamonds Snood', Michelle Griffiths (photo by Mark Cleghorn), see Textile Artists and Designers, p. 99

Information for overseas readers of the textile directory 2003

When telephoning or faxing UK numbers from overseas first dial the correct international prefix followed by 44. Then omit the first 0 of the number as listed.

Editor's Introduction

Thanks to the energy, enthusiasm and support of artists, businesses and organisations in the world of creative textiles, the first edition of *The Textile Directory* (2002) proved to be a huge success. Without exception, the specialist press considered it to be a 'must-have' for all and, as word spread, orders came flooding in from all over the country and all corners of the globe. And along with orders for copies came dozens of supportive and constructive messages. I would like to apologise to anyone who wrote in and didn't receive a personal letter back. All suggestions for inclusions were most gratefully received and followed up. We write to everyone we hear about, offering them a free listing. We send reminders by e-mail and sometimes we even telephone, but occasionally we receive no response. So as well as making suggestions, please help us by encouraging your contacts to take an entry. In the end it is a resource for everybody and the more inclusive it is, the better for all.

This year we are delighted to welcome Val Campbell-Harding as a guest writer. On page 64 she encourages us to explore taking up the challenge of one the new 7802 courses now available. Also in the editorial line, you will find an article on more informal courses and workshops on page 90.

With a final thanks to all of you who wrote, faxed, e-mailed and phoned, we present the brand new, bigger, bolder and better *Textile Directory 2003*! We hope you find all that you are looking for. (See below for some pointers to the main changes.) If, however, you notice anyone missing, have any suggestions or criticisms, again we would love to hear from you. The Directory will continue to be updated annually.

Sue Richardson, Editor

Using The Textile Directory 2003

At the end of most sections, where relevant, you will find a list of entries by geographical area. We hope you find this addition useful – please let us know.

We also include a list of diary dates on p. 24 featuring all the major shows and fairs of the year. If we've missed any, please call us!

NEW in this edition are major new sections of Mail Order Suppliers and Shops. These are split into smaller sections to help you find what you need, for example Embroidery, Knitting/Crochet, Patchwork and Quilting, etc. See p. 31 (Mail Order Suppliers) and p. 65 (Shops) for the page numbers of these specialist sub-sections.

This year we have a much more comprehensive general index with page numbers. If in doubt about how a person or company is listed in the Directory, look here first.

t This symbol indicates that the entrant has informed us that they provide some kind of tuition. This provision will vary, so you are advised to contact them for further details if you are interested in taking a class or course.

Copies of **The Textile Directory** are obtainable from:

Word4Word (Prop. Sue Richardson),
107 High Street, Evesham WR11 4EB

Published by Word4Word
Edited by: **Sue Richardson, Word4Word, Evesham UK**
Printed by: **Lemon Press, Redditch, UK**

ISBN 0-9541209-1-4

The Textile Directory, Word4Word, 107 High Street, Evesham WR11 4EB
t 0870 220 2423 **f** 01386 760401
e info@thetextiledirectory.com **w** www.thetextiledirectory.com

Contents

Index of Advertisers

Adult and Further Education

Alston Hall
Alston Lane, Longridge, Preston PR3 3BP
t 01772 784661 f 01772 785835
e alston.hall@ed.lancscc.gov.uk
w www.alstonhall.u-net.com
Residential day and evening courses including many textile related subjects. Beautiful location in the heart of the Ribble Valley.

ARCA (Adult Residential Colleges Assoc.)
PO Box 31, Washbrook, Ipswich IP8 3HP
t 01473 730737 f 01473 730737
e derek.barbanell@dial.pipex.com
w www.aredu.org.uk
Short (weekend, mid-week, one-week) courses in some 30 member colleges in England, Wales and Northern Ireland.

Askham Bryan College
Askham Bryan, York YO2 3PR
t 01904 772277 f 01904 772288
e sf@askham-bryan.ac.uk
w www.askham-bryan.ac.uk
Courses for all in patchwork and quilting, embroidery, soft furnishing, upholstery, silk painting, interior decorative techniques, interior design, textiles, bead weaving.

Barnfield College
Rotheram Avenue, Luton, Beds LU1 5PP
t 01582 569700 f 01582 569731
e anne.kemp@ra.barnfield.ac.uk
w www.barnfield.ac.uk
Creative courses leading to City & Guilds qualifications in embroidery, textile decoration, fashion, soft furnishing, patchwork, clothing. Phone for directory.

Belfast Institute of Further and Higher Education, Fashion and Textiles
College Square East, Belfast BT1 6DJ
t 028 9026 5037 f 028 9026 5001
Courses available: City & Guilds 7900 Fashion, 7900 Soft Furnishings, 7900 Embroidery.

Belstead House
Belstead, Ipswich, Suffolk IP8 3NA
t 01473 686321 f 01473 686664
e belstead.house@educ.suffolk.gov.uk
Short residential courses for adults in relaxed and comfortable surroundings. Wide choice of subjects available throughout the year.

Bolton Community College
Clarence Street, Bolton BL1 7HF
t 01204 333900 f 01204 333937
e joyce-read@msn.com
w www.bolton-community-college.ac.uk
From basic beginners to full City & Guilds in creative crafts at sites throughout the Bolton area.

Bradford College
School of Art, Design and Textiles, Lister Building, Great Horton Road, Bradford BD7 1AY
t 01274 751634 f 01274 753236
e admissions@bilk.ac.uk
w www.bilk.ac.uk
BTEC ND/NC Fashion Design 2 yrs, FT/PT; BA (Hons) Fashion Design FT/PT; BA (Hons) Textile Design FT/PT.

Bromley Adult Education College
Nightingale Lane, Bromley, Kent BR1 2SQ
t 020 8460 0020 f 020 8466 7299
e enquiries@bromleyadulteducation.ac.uk
w bromleyadulteducation.ac.uk
Part-time courses in: beadwork, dressmaking and pattern-cutting, embroidery, patchwork and quilting, rag rugging, soft furnishing and upholstery, lacemaking. See ad on p. 9.

Burton Manor College
The Village, Burton, Neston, Cheshire CH64 5SJ
t 0151 336 5172 f 0151 336 6586
e enquiry@burtonmanor.com
w www.burtonmanor.com
Wide variety of residential and day courses including: bead needle weaving; Japanese embroidery; luxurious velvets and sumptuous surfaces and many more!

Bury Lifelong Learning Service

Education Department, Athenaeum House, Market Street, Bury BL9 0BW
t 0161 253 7265 f 0161 253 7264
e g.hughes@bury.gov.uk
Offers a wide range of art/craft/textile courses over six centres covering the Borough of Bury.

Calderdale College

Percival Whitley Centre, Francis Street, Halifax, Yorkshire HX1 3UZ
t 01422 399331 f 01422 399396
e judye@calderdale.ac.uk
w www.calderdale.ac.uk
Our broad-based National Diploma in Textiles gives students the confidence to progress to higher education or textile-linked employment.

Cardonald College

690 Mosspark Drive, Glasgow G52 3AY
t 0141 272 3333 f 0141 272 3444
e enquiries@cardonald.ac.uk
w www.cardonald.ac.uk
Cardonald College offers a wide variety of qualifications ranging from HND in Stitched Textiles to City & Guilds in Embroidery, Millinery, Soft Furnishing and Feltmaking.

Chelmsford College

Moulsham Street, Chelmsford, Essex CM2 0JQ
t 01245 265611 f 01245 349009
A broad range of part-time courses for adults in many areas of craft/design. Beginners to advanced levels.

Coleg Gwent

Abergavenny 'the Hill' Campus, Pen-y-pound, Abergavenny, Monmouthshire NP7 7RP
t 01495 333777 f 01495 333778
e hill@coleggwent.ac.uk
w www.coleggwent.ac.uk
We offer a wide range of craft courses - day, weekend and summer school. Please phone us for full details.

Lesley Coles Cert. Ed. (FE)

47 Killyvarder Way, Boscoppa, St Austell, Cornwall PL25 3DJ
t 01726 61632
e lesley.coles@ntlworld.com
Qualified teacher of adults. Residential, monthly and weekly classes for beginners to experienced students - mainly in Cornwall. SAE for details. See also Textile Artists and Designers.

Community Education Lewisham

Brockley Rise Centre, 2 Brockley Rise, Deptford, London SE23 1PR
t 020 8690 5906 f 020 8314 1684
e etaylor@altavista.co.uk
w www.cel.lewisham.gov.uk
Basketry, beadwork, clothesmaking, crafts, lacemaking, patchwork, soft furnishing, tailoring, textile foundation, upholstery. Many other courses available. Please call for information.

Craven College

High Street, Skipton, North Yorkshire BD23 1JY
t 01756 791411
Creative textile courses including City & Guilds 7900 plus 7802 in Embroidery, Patchwork and Quilting. HND/HNC Textile Design plus many weekend courses.

Croydon Continuing Education and Training Service

Smitham CETS Centre, Malcolm Road, Couldsdon, Surrey CR5 2DB
t 0870 556 1630
w www.cets.co.uk
Providers of a wide variety of introductory, certificated and diploma courses in lacemaking, patchwork, embroidery, upholstery, soft furnishing and fashion.

Debden House Centre

Debden Green, Loughton, Essex IG10 2PA
t 020 8508 3008 f 020 8508 0284
An adult education centre in the heart of Epping Forest. Various courses available most weekends. Quilting a speciality!

Denman College

Marcham , Abingdon, Oxfordshire OX13 6NW
t 01865 391991 f 01865 391966
e info@denman.org.uk
w www.womens-institute.org.uk
Denman, the Women's Institute's adult residential college offering courses for WI members, Associate members and members of like-minded organisations.

Derby College
Prince Charles Avenue, Mackworth, Derby
DE22 4LR
t 01332 519951 **f** 01332 510548
*C&G Creative Skills 7802/Creative Studies
7900, Parts 1 & 2, Embroidery and
Patchwork/Quilting. Also BTEC National
Diploma in Fashion and Clothing.*

Dillington House
Ilminster, Somerset TA19 9DT
t 01460 52427 **f** 01460 52433
e dillington@somerset.gov.uk
w www.dillington.co.uk
*Residential centre offering a wide range of arts
and crafts courses including lacemaking,
needlecraft, embroidery and pictures from fabric.*

Eastleigh College
Cranbury Centre, Cranbury Annexe,
Cranbury Road, Eastleigh, Hants SO50 5HG
t 02380 322140 **f** 02380 362034
e cranbury@eastleigh.ac.uk
*City & Guilds Embroidery, Masterclass in
Stitched Textiles, Embroidery for Beginners,
Saturday workshops, Patchwork & Quilting and
other textile courses.*

Fareham College
Main Campus Adult Learning Centre,
Bishopsfield Road, Fareham PO14 1NH
t 01329 815200 **f** 01329 822483
e careers@fareham.ac.uk
w www.fareham.ac.uk
*Adult education classes in embroidery, dress-
making, bobbin lacemaking, patchwork & quilting,
soft furnishings, upholstery, machine embroidery.*

Ferndown Adult Education
Mountbatten Drive, Ferndown, Dorset
BH22 9EW
t 01202 875359 **f** 01202 861088
w www.adult-ed.co.uk
*A variety of textile courses including City &
Guilds Creative Studies: Patchwork and
Quilting.*

Furness College
Channelside, Barrow-in-Furness, Cumbria
LA14 2PJ
t 01229 825017 **f** 01229 870964
*Specialist textile courses - part-time leisure and
City & Guilds.*

Gloscat, Creative Textiles
Cheltenham Campus, Princess Elizabeth
Way, Cheltenham GL51 7SJ
t 01242 532000
e truemb@gloscat.ac.uk
*Full range of courses including City & Guilds
Embroidery, Fashion, Feltmaking, Soft
Furnishing, Patchwork and Quilting. Summer
School courses available.*

Gorseinon College
Belgrave Road, Gorseinon, Swansea SA4 6RD
t 01792 893054 **f** 01792 893675
e admin@gorseinon.ac.uk
*C&G 7802/7900 Embroidery, Fashion, Interior
Decorative Techniques, Machine Embroidery,
Costume Jewellery, Mixed Media, Batik,
Feltmaking, Printmaking, Costume Jewellery,
Creative Computing.*

Grantham College
Stonebridge Road, Grantham NG31 9AP
t 01476 400200 **f** 01476 400291
w www.grantham.ac.uk
*City & Guilds courses including Embroidery,
Silk Painting, Soft Furnishing.*

Grantley Hall
Ripon , North Yorkshire HG4 3ET
t 01765 620259 **f** 01765 620443
e grantley.hall@northyorks.gov.uk
*A variety of textile and other short courses
available all year in this magnificent setting in
North Yorkshire.*

Greenwich Community College
Royal Hill, Greenwich, London SE10 8PY
t 020 8858 2211 **f** 020 8293 9883
e info@gcc.ac.uk
w www.gcc.ac.uk
*Part-time day and evening classes in fashion and
textile crafts. A wide range of general interest,
access and C&G 7802 courses available.*

Guildford College
Stoke Park, Guildford, Surrey GU1 1EZ
t 01483 448500 **f** 01483 448603
e scross@guildford.ac.uk
w www.guildford.ac.uk
*Short textiles courses in a range of techniques
including silk painting, batik, tie-dye, weaving,
hand and machine embroidery, rug-making,
appliqué.*

Harrogate College
Hornbeam Park, Harrogate HG2 8QT
t 01423 879466 **f** 01423 879829
ND Textiles, fashion and clothing. City and Guilds Embroidery, Fashion. Students 19+ free tuition fees on full-time courses!

Hastings College of Arts and Technology
Archery Road, St Leonards on Sea, E Sussex TN38 0HX
t 01424 442222
e amsmith@hastings.ac.uk
BTEC National Diploma in Fashion/Clothing. Two-year course covering design, garment construction and printed textiles for the fashion industry.

Henrietta Parker Centre
Ray Road, West Molesey, Surrey KT8 2LG
t 020 8979 3378 **f** 020 8979 5961
C&G Embroidery 7900 Parts 1 & 2. Various C&G 7802 courses.

Higham Hall College
Bassenthwaite Lake, Cockermouth, Cumbria CA13 9SH
t 01768 776276 **f** 01768 776013
e admin@higham-hall.org.uk
w www.higham-hall.org.uk
A wide range of textile and embroidery courses in superb accommodation and surroundings in the Lake District.

Hillingdon Adult Education Centres
London Borough of Hillingdon, Frays Adult Education, 65 Harefield Road, Uxbridge, Middlesex UB8 1PJ
t 01895 634714
Soft furnishing, window dressing, beadwork, creative embroidery, crewel work, bobbin lace, tassels cords and crochet, patchwork courses available at various venues. See ad on p.10.

Huddersfield Technical College, Adult and Continuing Education
St James Road, Marsh, Huddersfield HD1 4QA
t 01484 453988/538454
Part-time City & Guilds courses in Embroidery, Patchwork and Quilting and Creative Computing.

Inkberrow Design Centre
The Westall Centre, Holberrow Green, Nr Redditch B97 6JY
t 01386 793793 **f** 01386 793364
e Brenda@idcink.fsnet.co.uk
An accredited City and Guilds Centre of Excellence for Fashion, Millinery, Embroidery, Theatrical Costume, Pattern Cutting and Floristry. Some courses are free. See also Art and Craft Centres; Private Colleges and Workshop Organisers.

Knuston Hall
Irchester, Wellingborough, Northamptonshire NN29 7EU
t 01933 312104 **f** 01933 357596
e enquiries@knustonhall.org.uk
w www.knustonhall.org.uk
Residential study breaks in a wide variety of subjects – weekend, one-day and summer school (5- and 7-day courses).

Leicester Adult Education College
Wellington Street, Leicester LE1 6HL
t 0116 233 4343 **f** 0116 233 4344
e admin@leicester-adult-ed.ac.uk
w www.leicester-adult-ed.ac.uk
The college offers a wide range of textile courses, from beginners to City & Guilds Creative Studies Parts 1 & 2.

Lewisham College
Breakspears Building, Lewisham Way, London SE4 1UT
t 020 8692 0353 **f** 020 8694 9163
e info@lewisham.ac.uk
w www.lewisham.ac.uk
BTEC National Diploma Textiles - a broad-based, varied, innovative course covering many approaches to generating ideas, designing and making work.

Longslade Community College
Wanlip Lane, Birstall, Leicester LE4 4GH
t 0116 267 3389 **f** 0116 267 4510
w www.longslade.freeserve.co.uk
Adult education including C&G Creative Embroidery and Masterclass. Art, crafts, computers and general interest.

Malvern Hills College

Malvern Hills College, Albert Road North, Malvern, Worcestershire WR14 2YH
t 01684 565351 **f** 01684 561767
e malvernhills@lineone.net
A wide range of textile and embroidery courses, including recreational, City & Guilds, OCN and degree-level modules. See also Summer Schools.

Maryland College

Leighton Street, Woburn, Beds MK17 9JD
t 01525 292901 **f** 01525 290856
e twissv@maryland.bedfordshire.gov.uk
Delightful college in Woburn offering many weekend residential short course and day events. Free brochure.

Middlesbrough College

Roman Road, Middlesbrough TS5 5PJ
t 01642 813706
Wide range of City & Guilds and NCFE courses including Fashion, Embroidery, Patchwork, Soft Furnishing, Upholstery, Millinery.

Missenden Abbey Adult Learning

Great Missenden, Bucks HP16 0BN
t 01494 862904 **f** 01494 890087
e conedchil@buckscc.gov.uk
w www.aredu.org.uk/missendenabbey
Residential and non-residential weekends and Summer School in the beautiful Chiltern Hills. Wide range of textiles courses available all year. See ad on p. 10.

New College Durham

Framwellgate Moor, Durham DH1 5ES
t 0191 375 4318 **f** 0191 375 4222
e maggie.smith@newdur.ac.uk
A full range of City & Guilds Creative Textile/Design courses, day/evening, flexible learning packages and leisure courses are available.

North and West Essex Adult Community College

Northbrooks House, Northbrooks, Harlow, Essex CM19 4DS
t 01279 436230 **f** 01279 436230
e enquiry@nweacc.ac.uk
w www.nweacc.ac.uk
The college offers a large variety of courses including City & Guilds Creative Studies and other textile classes.

North East Surrey College of Technology (NESCOT)

Reigate Road, Ewell, Epsom, Surrey KT17 3DS
t 020 8394 1731 **f** 020 8394 3030
e lcoope@nescot.ac.uk **w** www.nescot.ac.uk
City & Guilds Creative Studies.

North Essex Adult Community College

c/o John Bramston School, Spinks Lane, Witham, Essex CM8 1EP
t 01376 516533 **f** 01376 513099
e neacc@essexcc.gov.uk
The college provides C&G PWD, Embroidery Parts 1 & 2 and plans to add 7702 and 7802 in the near future.

North Lindsey College

Kingsway, Scunthorpe, North Lincolnshire DN17 1AJ
t 01724 281111 **f** 01724 294020
e info@northlindsey.ac.uk
w www.northlindsey.ac.uk
Good range of full-time courses in art and design plus part-time day and evening classes.

North Warwickshire and Hinkley College, Nuneaton

Hinckley Road, Nuneaton, Warks CV11 6BH
t 02476 243000 **f** 02476 329056
e the.college@nwarks_hinckley.ac.uk
We offer a range of exciting courses: embroidery, textile design, fashion, soft furnishing and uphol-stery (City & Guilds and BTEC).

Northbrook College

Union Place, Elm Lawn House, Worthing, Sussex BN11 1LG
t 01903 606100 **f** 01903 606106
e adulteducation@nbcol.ac.uk
The college offers C&G 7900 Part 1 and Part 2 Embroidery, 7702 and 7802 Machine Embroidery, Textile masterclass. Tutor Sue Munday.

Oxford College of Further Education

Oxpens Road, Oxford OX1 1SA
t 01865 245871 **f** 01865 248871
e enquiries@oxfordcollege.ac.uk
w www.oxfordcollege.ac.uk
Full-time and part-time courses in Fashion/Textiles, including BTEC ND/NC in Fashion & Clothing and Textiles, and C&G Fashion 7822, 7922 & 7923.

Pyke House Residential Education Centre

Upper Lake, Battle, East Sussex TN33 0AN
t 01424 772495 **f** 01424 775041
e Hcatpykehouse@btinternet.com
Offering textile tuition in a relaxed, friendly environment. Regular residential courses include bobbin lace, patchwork, goldwork and fabric box making.

Redbridge Institute of Adult Education

Gaysham Avenue, Gants Hill, Ilford, Essex
IG2 6TD
t 020 8550 2398 **f** 020 8551 7584
e enquiries@redbridge-iae.ac.uk
w www.redbridge-iae.ac.uk
Courses in creative textiles including Machine Embroidery, Patchwork and Quilting and Textile Printing. An extensive range of related courses also available. See ad on p. 10.

Richmond Adult Community College

Clifden Road, Twickenham TW1 4LT
t 020 8891 5907 **f** 020 8332 5660
e ann.israel@racc.ac.uk
w www.racc.ac.uk
70 textile and fashion courses. Beginners to City & Guilds. Printing, dyeing, embroidery, feltmaking, quilting, millinery, pattern cutting, clothesmaking, etc.

Rowan and Jaeger Handknits

Green Lane Mill, Holmfirth, W Yorks
HD9 2DX
t 01484 681881 **f** 01484 687920
e mail@knitrowan.com
w www.knitrowan.com
The best in handknitting design with a range of knitting magazines, beautiful yarns and knitting courses nationwide. See also Mail Order Suppliers (Knitting/Crochet); Publications; Websites.

Sandwell College of Further and Higher Education

Pound Road, Woden Road South, Oldbury,
W Midlands B68 8NA
t 0800 622006 **f** 0121 253 6836
e enquiries@sandwell.ac.uk
w www.sandwell.ac.uk
Sandwell College offers a wide range of programmes, including nationally recognised qualifications in fashion, textiles and related areas.

School of Arts, City College, Coventry

The Butts, Coventry CV1 3DG
t 02476 526700 **f** 02476 526789
e info@covcollege.ac.uk
w www.covcollege.ac.uk
City & Guilds Embroidery, Parts I & II, HNC Surface Pattern/Textiles, HNC Spatial Design/Interiors.

South Nottingham College

Farnborough Rd, Clifton, Nottingham
NG11 8LU
t 0115 914 6300/6471 **f** 0115 914 6333
e enquiries@south-nottingham.ac.uk
w www.south-nottingham.ac.uk
A wide choice of vocational textile courses, day or evening which may be combined for full-time attendance.

South Trafford College

Manchester Road, West Timperley,
Altrincham, Cheshire WA14 5PQ
t 0161 952 4600 **f** 0161 952 4672
e ashep@stcoll.ac.uk
w www.stcoll.ac.uk
Creative courses - non-vocational and City & Guilds. All levels in Embroidery, Patchwork & Quilting, Fashion, Textile Techniques, Computer Design and others.

Southampton City College

St Mary Street, Southampton, Hampshire
SO14 1AR
t 023 8048 4848 **f** 023 8057 7473
e information@southampton-city.ac.uk
w www.southampton-city.ac.uk
National Diploma Fashion and Clothing, Textiles, City & Guilds 7900 Embroidery, Dressmaking, Patchwork & Quilting, OCN Patchwork & Quilting.

Southend Adult Community College

Southchurch Centre, Ambleside Drive,
Southend on Sea, Essex SS1 2UP
t 01702 445700 **f** 01702 445739
e info@southend-adult.co.uk
w www.southend-adult.ac.co.uk
Part-time courses: feltmaking, printed textiles, lacemaking, weaving, C&G Patchwork, GCE A level, ncfe Victorian Crafts and Soft Furnishing, plus summer activities.

Stoke on Trent College (Burslem Site)

Burslem School of Art, Queen Street,
Burslem, Stoke on Trent, Staffs ST6 3EJ
t 01782 208208
*A variety of textile courses, including OCN,
National Certificate in Art & Craft and AS/A
level Textiles.*

Stourbridge College

Hagley Rd, Stourbridge, W Midlands DY8 1QU
t 01384 344344
*Courses offered: HNC in Textile Design,
National Diplomas in Textiles, Fashion and
Clothing, plus extensive City and Guilds creative
programme.*

Sussex Downs College, Eastbourne Campus

Cross Levels Way, Eastbourne BN21 2UF
t 01323 637637 **f** 01323 637472
e info@ecat.ac.uk
w www.ecat.ac.uk
*Part-time day and evening courses in printed
and stitched textiles including C&G Creative
Studies Parts 1& 2 in Embroidery and
Patchwork & Quilting.*

Thrunscoe Adult Education Centre

Highgate, Cleethorpes,
North East Lincolnshire
t 01472 609094 **f** 01472 603298
e lynne.maultby@nelincs.gov.uk
*C&G creative courses: Design, Embroidery,
P&Q, Feltmaking, Creative Computing, Lace,
Painting and Drawing, Mixed Media/Design,
Theatre Costume, Soft Furnishing.*

Tresham Institute of Further and Higher Education

Room A104, Windmill Avenue Campus,
Kettering, Northants NN15 6ER
t 01536 413244/0845 6588990
w www.tresham.ac.uk
*City & Guilds Creative Studies in Embroidery
and Patchwork and Quilting: 7802, 7900 Part 1
and Part 2.*

Tunbridge Wells Adult Education Centre

Monson Road, Tunbridge Wells, Kent TN1 1LS
t 01892 527317 **f** 01892 529743
w www.kent.gov.uk/adulted
*All our tutors are experienced practitioners who
are committed to adult learning.*

University of Central Lancashire, Cumbria Campus at Newton Rigg

Newton Rigg, Penrith, Cumbria CA11 0AH
t 01768 863791 **f** 01768 867249
e info@newtonrigg.ac.uk
w www.newtonrigg.ac.uk
*City & Guilds 7900 (Parts 1& 2) and 7802
Creative Studies - Embroidery, Patchwork and
Quilting, Soft Furnishings, Upholstery. High-
quality, innovative approach.*

Urchfont Manor College

Urchfont, Devizes, Wiltshire SN10 4RG
t 01380 840495 **f** 01380 840005
e urchfont@wccyouth.org.uk
w www.aredu.org.uk
*Offering a range of residential leisure and study
breaks. Days, weeks and weekends. Also
conference facilities available for hire.*

Walsall College of Arts and Technology (WALCAT)

College of Arts and Technology, St Pauls
Street, Walsall, W Midlands WS1 1XN
t 01922 657000/058 **f** 01922 657083
e jrevill@walcat.ac.uk
w www.walcat.ac.uk
*BTEC National Diploma Fashion, Interior
Design, HND Fashion, Millinery, Embroidery,
Soft Furnishings, Printmaking.*

Wansfell College

30 Piercing Hill, Theydon Bois, Essex
CM16 7LF
t 01992 813027 **f** 01992 814761
e education@wansfellcollege.net
w www.wansfellcollege.net
*Residential mid-week and weekend courses in a
wide range of subjects. Also available as a venue
for training courses.*

Warwickshire College, Leamington Spa and Moreton Morrell

Warwick New Road, Leamington Spa,
Warwickshire CV32 5JE
t 01926 318000 **f** 01926 319025
e dhirons@warkscol.ac.uk
*Full- and part-time courses throughout the year
in textiles and related disciplines. Awarding
bodies include OCN, City & Guilds and Edexcel.*

Wensum Lodge

169 King Street, Norwich NR1 1QW
t 01603 666021 f 01603 765633
e wensum.adult.edu@norfolk.gov.uk
Short and long courses in embroidery, beading, painting on silk, crochet and bobbin lace. City-centre location. Residential accommodation often available.

West Dean College

Chichester, West Sussex PO18 0QZ
t 01243 811301 f 01243 811343
e enquiries@westdean.org.uk
w www.westdean.org.uk
Short courses in textile media (embroidery, stitch, painting, printing, dyeing, weaving, lace-making and other techniques). Postgraduate diplomas in tapestry weaving. See also Higher Education/Research Centres; Private Colleges and Workshop Organisers; Textile Artists and Designers.

Westhope College

Westhope, Craven Arms, Shropshire SY7 9JL
t 01584 861293 f 01584 861 293
e learn@westhope.org.uk
w www.westhope.org.uk
Classes for adults in a wide range of crafts, all levels, weekends and one-day, from lace to pottery to patchwork.

Wiltshire College Trowbridge

College Road, Trowbridge, Wiltshire
BA14 0ES
t 01225 766241 f 01225 777148
e booteb@wiltscoll.ac.uk
w www.wiltscoll.ac.uk
We deliver high quality City & Guilds craft tuition with good facilities and offer 8 7802 and 5 7900 qualifications.

Windsor School of Textile Art

East Berkshire College, Claremont Road, Windsor, Berkshire SL4 3AZ
t 01753 793000 f 01753 793119
w www.eastberks.ac.uk
Exciting and creative embroidery, patchwork & quilting courses for all levels, from beginners to Diploma in Stitched Textiles.

Worcester College of Technology

School of Art and Design, Barbourne Road, Worcester WR1 1RT
t 01905 725631
e smaund@wortech.ac.uk
w www.wortech.ac.uk
Full-time National Diploma in Textiles and Art and Design Foundation course (full-time/part-time). Informal classes in smocking, quilting, embroidery at 28 The Cross, Worcester, t 01905 726002.

Colleges listed by area

East Anglia

Belstead House
Grantham College
North and West Essex Adult Community College
North Essex Adult Community College
Wensum Lodge

Midlands

Derby College
Gloscat, Creative Textiles
Inkberrow Design Centre
Knuston Hall
Leicester Adult Education College
Longslade Community College
Malvern Hills College
North Warwickshire and Hinkley College, Nuneaton
Sandwell College of Further and Higher Education
School of Arts, City College, Coventry
South Nottingham College
Stoke on Trent College (Burslem Site)
Stourbridge College
Tresham Institute of Further and Higher Education
Walsall College of Arts and Technology (WALCAT)

Warwickshire College, Leamington Spa and Moreton Morrell
Westhope College
Worcester College of Technology

North Central

Grantley Hall
Harrogate College

North East

Askham Bryan College
Bradford College
Craven College
Middlesbrough College
New College Durham
North Lindsey College
Thrunscoe Adult Education Centre

North West

Alston Hall
Bolton Community College
Burton Manor College
Bury Lifelong Learning Service
Calderdale College

North West cont.

Furness College
Higham Hall College
Huddersfield Technical College
Rowan and Jaeger Handknits
South Trafford College
University of Central Lancashire, Cumbria Campus at
  Newton Rigg

Northern Ireland

Belfast Institute of Further and Higher Education,
  Fashion and Textiles

Scotland

Cardonald College

South Central

Eastleigh College
Fareham College
Southampton City College
West Dean College

South East

Barnfield College
Bromley Adult Education College
Chelmsford College
Community Education Lewisham
Croydon Continuing Education and Training Service
Debden House Centre
Denman College
Greenwich Community College

Guildford College
Hastings College of Arts and Technology
Henrietta Parker Centre
Hillingdon Adult Education Centres
Lewisham College
Maryland College
Missenden Abbey Adult Learning
North East Surrey College of Technology (NESCOT)
Northbrook College
Oxford College of Further Education
Pyke House Residential Education Centre
Redbridge Institiue of Adult Education
Richmond Adult Community College
Southend Adult Community College
Sussex Downs College, Eastbourne Campus
Tunbridge Wells Adult Education Centre
Wansfell College
Windsor School of Textile Art

South West

Lesley Coles Cert. Ed. (FE)
Dillington House
Ferndown Adult Education
Urchfont Manor College
Wiltshire College Trowbridge

UK

ARCA (Adult Residential Colleges Association)

Wales

Coleg Gwent
Gorseinon College

Creative Courses Available

H illingdon
A dult
E ducation

Soft Furnishings with Cane Seating starting September 2002, Thursdays am & pm, Harlington Adult Education Centre, *0208 569 1613*

Window Dressing C & G Thursday evening, Harlington Adult Education Centre, *0208 569 1613*

Counted Beadwork Saturday 23rd Nov 2002 for the day at Frays Adult Ed. Centre , *01895 254766*

Counted Beadwork Saturday 8th March 2003 for the day at Harlington Centre, *0208 569 1613*

Creative Embroidery from January and April, Wednesday mornings at Frays Adult Education Centre, Uxbridge, *01895 254766*

Embroidery – Crewel in January, Friday mornings at Frays Ad. Ed. Centre, *01895 254766*

Bobbin Lace Tuesday and Wednesday mornings at Frays Ad. Ed. Centre, *01895 254766*

Tassels, Cords and Crochet starting 7th March 2003, Friday afternoons, 18 weeks, at Frays Ad. Ed. Centre, *01895 254766*

Crazy Patchwork 2nd November 01 - 9.30, one day at Frays Ad. Ed. Centre, *01895 254766*

Plus - many other courses available

Making a difference

Frays Adult Education. 65 Harefield Road, Uxbridge, Middlesex. UB8 1PJ

Antiques/Auctions/Conservation

Bonhams

The Old House, Station Road, Knowle,
Solihull, West Midlands B93 0HT
t 01564 776151 **f** 01564 776151
e samantha.lilley@bonhams.com
w www.bonhams.com
*Bonham's International Textile Department will
hold 4 sales per year, featuring antique lace,
embroideries, textiles, costume, haute couture
and fans.*

John Gillow

50 Gwydir Street, Cambridge CB1 2LL
t 01223 313803
Oriental and African textiles.

Malcolm Welch

Wild Jebbett, Pudding Bag Lane, Thurlaston,
Rugby CV23 9JZ
t 01788 810616
e malcolm.welch4@virgin.net
*Pre-1960s buttons, lace magazines from the
1900s through 1940. Antique lace bobbins, both
bone and wooden. Please email me.*

Sonia Cordell Antiques

Snape Maltings Antique Centre, Snape,
Suffolk IP17 1SR and Woodbridge Gallery,
Woodbridge, Suffolk IP1 4LX
t 01394 282254
*Antique needlework tools, thimbles, scissors,
shuttles to originally fitted boxes. Happy to buy
similar items. Search service offered.*

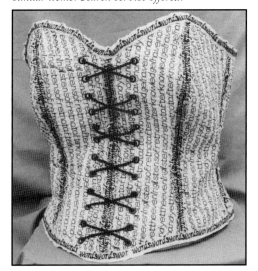

Textile Cleaning & Conservation

271 Sandown Road, Deal, Kent CT14 6QU
t 01304 373684 **f** 01304 373684
e condore@btinternet.com
*Highly specialised cleaning of woven, printed
and embroidered textiles, fans, lace, upholstery,
costume. Advice on display and storage for
collections.*

(The) Textile Restoration Studio

2 Talbot Road, Bowdon, Altrincham,
Cheshire WA14 3JD
t 0161 928 0020 **f** 0161 928 0020
e enquiries@textilerestoration.co.uk
w www.textilerestoration.co.uk
*Conservation/restoration of antique embroidery,
lace, costume, ecclesiastical and woven textiles.
Consultancy advice, specialist courses and
products available. See also Private Colleges and
Workshop Organisers.*

(The) Thimble Society

PO Box 25362, London NW5 4ZW
t 020 7419 9562 **f** 020 7419 9562
w www.thimblesociety.co.uk
*Founded on a family-shared passion for sewing
related objects. Quarterly magazine with
thimbles to buy, articles, restoring tips, etc.*

Body of Knowledge, 2001, Elli Woodsford, The
Embroidery Exchange, see Websites, p. 109

Art and Craft Centres

2 Fish Gallery
Gissing Road, Burston, Nr Diss, Norfolk
IP22 5UD
t 01379 741796 **f** 01379 740711
e twofishgallery@hotmail.com
*We show furniture by David Gregson and
ceramics, textiles, jewellery, sculpture, glass, etc
by local craftsmen (many Suffolk Craft
Society members).*

Blakemere Craft Centre
Chester Road, Sandiway, Northwich,
Cheshire CW8 2EB
t 01606 883261 **f** 01606 301495
e info@blakemerecrafts.co.uk
w www.blakemere-shoppingexperience.com
*Over 30 shops in Edwardian stables. Huge
selection of gifts, crafts, furniture. Garden centre,
children's playbarn, aquatic/falconry centre,
restaurant/coffee shop.*

Bolton Play Resource Centre
Leonard Street, Bolton, Lancashire BL3 3AP
t 01204 334040 **f** 01204 334420
e resource.centre@bolton.gov.uk
*Provider of quality, low cost craft materials
to everyone working with children and
young people.*

Broadland Arts Centre **t**
The Old School, Dilham, North Walsham,
Norfolk NR28 9PS
t 01702 475361/01692 536486 **f** 01702 475361
e bac@dammery.freeserve.co.uk
w www.broadlandarts.co.uk
*Varied textile courses from March to November
with world-class tutors. Jan Beaney, Jean
Littlejohn, Janet Edmonds. Chinese trip autumn
2003.*

Cajobah Gallery **t**
Contemporary Craft Gallery, 3 Hamilton
Square, Birkenhead, Wirral CH41 6AU
t 0151 647 9577 **f** 0151 647 9577
*Specialist contemporary textile gallery with
monthly exhibition calendar. Shop selling art &
craft gifts and cards. Tearoom facilities. Free
admission. See also Private Colleges and
Workshop Organisers.*

Church Meadow Crafts
Lady Heyes Craft Centre, Kingsley Road,
Frodsham, Cheshire WA6 6SU
t 01606 594200
e lynn@lacemaking.co.uk
*Full range of lacemaking equipment - pillows,
bobbins, threads, etc. and cross-stitch and
embroidery supplies for beginner to expert.*

Cockington Court Craft Centre
Cockington Court, Cockington Village,
Torquay, Devon TQ2 6XA
t 01803 606035 **f** 01803 690391
e info@countryside-trust.org.uk
w www.countryside-trust.org.uk
*Cockington Court Craft Studios are hidden away
within a beautiful secret valley. Come and see the
craftspeople at work.*

(The) Court Cupboard Craft Gallery **t**
New Court Farm, Llantilio Pertholey,
Abergavenny, Monmouthshire NP7 8AU
t 01873 852011
*Sales galleries, exhibition space and
workshops housed in converted barns in
picturesque rural setting near Abergavenny.
Open daily 10.30-5.00.*

Dowally Craft Centre
Dowally, By Pitlochry, Perthshire PH9 0NT
t 01350 727604
*An Aladdin's cave of quality crafts and gifts plus
Dowally pottery, quilted hangings and stencilled
boxes made in the centre.*

(The) Grace Barrand Design Centre **t**
19 High Street, Nutfield, Surrey RH1 4HH
t 01737 822865 **f** 01737 822617
e info@gbdc.co.uk
w www.gbdc.co.uk
*A shop and gallery selling contemporary design
with a changing programme of exhibitions, plus
art-based courses and workshops.*

Inkberrow Design Centre

The Westall Centre, Holberrow Green,
Nr Redditch B97 6JY
t 01386 793793 **f** 01386 793364
e Brenda@idcink.fsnet.co.uk
Youth Designer Fashion Clubs, 8 to 16 years.
Also daytime, evening and weekend courses in
all aspects of Embroidery, Fashion, Millinery.
See also Adult and Further Education; Private
Colleges and Workshop Organisers.

(The) Jinney Ring Craft Centre

Hanbury, Bromsgrove B60 4BU
t 01527 821272 **f** 01527 821869
e greatwood@jinneyring.freeserve.co.uk
w www.jinneyringcraft.co.uk
Take a step back in time and visit a true craft
centre where craftspeople can be seen working.

Patchings Farm Art Centre

Oxton Road, Calverton, Nottingham
NG14 6NU
t 0115 965 3479 **f** 0115 965 5308
e info@patchingsartcentre.co.uk
w www.patchingsartcentre.co.uk
Classes and studio workshops in many textile
aspects. Annual textile exhibition. National
textile artists attend Art Festival in June.

Queens Park Centre

Queens Park, Aylesbury, Bucks HP21 7RT
t 01296 424332 **f** 01296 337363
e qpc@ukonline.co.uk
w www.qpc.org
Provides weekly workshops in embroidery,
patchwork, appliqué and dressmaking. Also
full- day special textile workshops with
professional artists.

Walford Mill Craft Centre

Stone Lane, Wimborne, Dorset BH21 1NL
t 01202 841400 **f** 01202 840132
e info@walford-mill.demon.co.uk
w www.walford-mill.co.uk
We have an exciting range of craft work in our
exhibitions, craft shop and workshops. We also
run educational classes.

Art and Craft Centres listed by area

East Anglia
2 Fish Gallery
Broadland Arts Centre

Midlands
Inkberrow Design Centre
Patchings Farm Art Centre
The Jinney Ring Craft Centre

North West
Blakemere Craft Centre
Bolton Play Resource Centre
Cajobah Gallery
Church Meadow Crafts

Scotland
Dowally Craft Centre

South East
(The) Grace Barrand Design Centre
Queens Park Centre

South West
Cockington Court Craft Centre
Walford Mill Craft Centre

Wales
The Court Cupboard Craft Gallery

13

Art Galleries and Exhibitions

art.tm
20 Bank Street, Inverness IV1 1QU
t 01463 712240 f 01463 239991
e info@arttm.org.uk
w www.arttm.org.uk
One of the Highlands' leading venues for contemporary visual arts and one of the country's most northerly Crafts Council approved outlets.

Art Van Go ⓪
The Studios, 1 Stevenage Road, Knebworth, Hertfordshire SG3 6AN
t 01438 814946 f 01438 816267
e art@artvango.co.uk
w www.artvango.co.uk
Continuously changing display of eclectic work, plus varied programme of dedicated exhibitions - jewellery, watercolours, textiles, embroidery, ceramics, etc. See also Mail Order Suppliers (Art Materials; Dyes/Silk Paints); Private Colleges and Workshop Organisers; Shops (Art Materials; Dyes/Silk Paints); ad on inside front cover.

Bevere Vivis Gallery & Picture Framers ⓪
Bevere Lane, Bevere, Worcester WR3 7RQ
t 01905 754484 f 01905 340215
e gallery@beverevivis.com
w www.beverevivis.com
Constantly changing exhibitions of painting and 3D art by up and coming and professional artists. Complete creative framing services.

Black Swan Arts
Frome, Somerset BA11 1BB
t 01373 473980 f 01373 451733
e ann@blackswan.org.uk
w www.blackswan.org.uk
A contemporary arts and crafts venue. There are two galleries dedicated to an ambitious programme of exhibitions all year round.

Bromham Mill Gallery
Bromham Mill, Bridge End, Bedford MK43 8LP
t 01234 824330 f 01234 824330
e bromhmill@deed.bedfordshire.gov.uk
w borneo.co.uk/bromham_mill
Contemporary textile gallery showing changing exhibitions of work, much of which is for sale. Other exhibitions, shop, watermill, refreshments.

C2+ Textile Gallery
33 Clerkenwell Green, London EC1R 0DU
t 020 7251 9200 f 020 7251 5655
e gallery@lesleycraze.demon.co.uk
w www.lesleycrazegallery.co.uk
Displays work by over 20 British textile artists. It is an informal gallery space and all work is for sale.

Church House Designs
Broad Street, Congresbury, Bristol BS19 5DG
t 01934 833660
We specialise in ceramics, glass, woodware and textiles, selected for quality by the Crafts Council. Phone for future exhibitions.

Collins Gallery ⓪
University of Strathclyde, 22 Richmond Street, Glasgow G1 1XQ
t 0141 548 2558 f 0141 552 4053
e collinsgallery@strath.ac.uk
w www.collinsgallery.strath.ac.uk
Jilli Blackwood: The Joy of Living. Major installation of textile art for the home, complemented by workshops. 23 August - 11 October 2003. See ad on p. 13.

Cotswold Heritage Centre ⓪
Fosseway, Northleach, Glos GL54 3JH
t 01451 860715
Ragrug-making demonstrations; classes; and tools for sale. Exhibitions.

Elizabeth Sykes Batiks
Islay House Square, Bridgend, Isle of Islay, PA44 7NZ
t 01496 810147 f 01496 810147
e ehs@islatran.demon.co.uk
w www.islatran.demon.co.uk
Studio/gallery where batik pictures are created and displayed. Also framed and unframed prints, greetings cards, scarves and much more.

Enigma Contemporary Art & Crafts
15 Vicarage St, Frome, Somerset BA11 1PX
t 01373 452079 f 01373 469810
e jen_enigma@fsbdial.co.uk
w www.enigma-gallery.com
A friendly venue consisting of the Main Gallery, Intimate Georgian Room, Sculpture Garden and Ceramic Studio. Ongoing programme of exhibitions.

Fabrications
No 7 Broadway Market, Hackney, London
E8 4PH
t 020 7275 8043 **f** 020 7275 8043
e textiles@fabrications1.co.uk
w www.fabrications1.co.uk
*Contemporary textile gallery/outlet showcasing
new and established designers' and artists' work
through monthly changing selling exhibitions.
Commissioning service available.*

Forge Mill Needle Museum
Needle Mill Lane, Riverside, Redditch,
Worcestershire B98 8HY
t 01527 62509 **f** 01527 66721
e museum@redditchbc.gov.uk
w www.redditchbc.gov.uk
*Exhibitions of contemporary textiles. Also runs
the annual Charles Henry Foyle Trust National
Needlework Competition. Contact the museum
for details. See also Museums; Shops (General
Needlecraft).*

Gosport Gallery
Walpole Road, Gosport, Hampshire
PO12 1NS
t 023 9258 8035 **f** 023 9250 8035
e musmop@hants.gov.uk
w www.hants.gov.uk/museum/gosport
*Creative textiles provide an important element
of the exhibitions programme for the Gosport
Gallery. Contact the museum or website
for details.*

Joss Graham Oriental Textiles
10 Eccleston Street, London SW1W 9LT
t 020 7730 4370 **f** 020 7730 4370
e jossgrahamgallery@btopenworld.com
*Well-known central London textile shop/gallery
featuring regular exhibitions devoted to world
textiles – often accompanied by creative
textile workshops.*

Lady Lever Art Gallery
Port Sunlight Village, Wirral CH62 5EQ
t 0151 478 4136
w www.ladyleverartgallery.org.uk
*A national treasure waiting to be explored.
Beautiful collections of 18th-century furniture,
Chinese porcelain, Wedgwood potteries
and tapestries.*

Llantarnam Grange Arts Centre
St David's Road, Cwmbran, Torfaen
NP44 1PD, Wales
t 01633 483321 **f** 01633 860584
e art@llantarnamgrange.fsnet.co.uk
*Small gallery showing art and craft by local,
national and international artists. Workshop
programme for adult, children and schools.*

(The) Minerva Art Centre
High Street, Llanidloes, Powys, Mid-Wales
SY18 6BX
t 01686 413467
e quilt.org.uk
*Gallery with changing exhibitions throughout
the year. Workshops and demonstrations, books,
cards and quilts old and new on sale.*

(The) New Studio
Rose Court, Olney, Bucks MK46 4BY
t 01234 711994 **f** 01234 241405
e keren@thenewstudio.co.uk
w www.thenewstudio.co.uk
*Occasional exhibitions of contemporary textile
work. Always willing to meet new artists.*

Percy House Gallery
38-42 Market Place, Cockermouth, Cumbria
CA13 9NG
t 01900 829667
w www.percyhouse.co.uk
*A large selection of contemporary arts by a wide
range of artists, situated in one of Cockermouth's
oldest town houses.*

Regatta Fine Art
2B Shirehall Plain, Holt, Norfolk NR25 6HZ
t 01263 710796
e Regatta-Fine-Art@Get-The-Web.com
w www.Regatta-Fine-Art.co.uk
*Regular changing work by contemporary artists
including mixed textile shows from around the
UK, jewellery, and the work of Ann McTavish.*

Ruthin Craft Centre, The Gallery
Park Road, Ruthin, Denbighshire,
North Wales LL15 1BB
t 01824 704774 **f** 01824 702060
*North Wales' premier centre for the applied arts
and craft. Changing programme of exhibitions
and workshops including textiles. Open daily.*

Shipley Art Gallery
Prince Consort Road, Gateshead NE8 4JB
t 0191 477 1495 **f** 0191 478 7917
e shipley@tyne-wear-museums.org.uk
Free entry gallery. Permanent collections,
including contemporary craft. Broad programme
of activities, education and courses, and
exhibitions (including textiles).

Wheelwrights Tea Rooms
14 Rodden Row, Abbotsbury, Dorset DT3 4JL
t 01305 871800
e suenigel@wheelwrights.co.uk
w www.wheelwrights.co.uk
Village tearoom - home-made cakes - exhibitions
by textile artists - 'Small Wall' gallery of textile
art. Open Wed-Sun 10.30-5.00.

Art Galleries by area

East Anglia
Regatta Fine Art

Midlands
Bevere Vivis Gallery
Forge Mill Needle
   Museum

North East
Shipley Art Gallery

North West
Lady Lever Art Gallery
Percy House Gallery

Scotland
art.tm
Collins Gallery
Elizabeth Sykes Batiks

South East
Art Van Go
Bromham Mill Gallery

C2+ Textile Gallery
Fabrications
Gosport Gallery
Joss Graham Oriental
   Textiles
The New Studio

South West
Black Swan Arts
Church House Designs
Cotswold Heritage
   Centre
Enigma Contemporary
   Art & Crafts
Wheelwrights Tea
   Rooms

Wales
Llantarnam Grange
   Arts Centre
(The) Minerva Art
Centre
Ruthin Craft Centre,
   The Gallery

Beads, Beads, Beads

21st Century Beads
Craft Workshops, South Pier Rd, Ellesmere Port, Merseyside CH65 4FW
t 0151 356 444 f 0151 355 3377
e sales@beadmaster.com
w www.beadmaster.com
Vast range of loose beads, findings, wires and threads. Mail-order catalogue available or call to our shop.

(The) Bead Merchant
PO Box 5025, Coggeshall, Essex, CO6 1HW
t 01376 563567 f 01376 563568
e info@beadmerchant.co.uk
w www. beadmerchant.co.uk
Specialists in beadwork kits for the beginner, and colour/texture theme packs for beadworkers and embroiderers. Beautiful beads catalogue £6.00. See ad on p. 20.

(The) Beadwork Company
19 Milton Avenue, Westcott, Dorking, Surrey RH4 3QA
t 01306 876526 f 01306 742193
e rosie@beadwork.net
w www.beadwork.net
Specialises in organising, promoting, setting up and running beadwork and beadwork-related textile workshops, exhibitions and fairs around the UK.

Beady Babas
8 Swan Court, East St, Andover, Hampshire SP10 1EZ
t 01264 339292
Huge range of beads and crystals, jewellery made on premises, incense, ethnic clothes and objets d'art, tarot cards, singing bowls.

Beechwood Beads
10 Beechwood Cres, Kirriemuir, Angus, Scotland DD8 5EE
t 01575 573401
e tich@globalnet.co.uk
A small mail order company based in Kirriemuir, Scotland, specialising in accent beads, Miyuki seed beads and beading accessories.

Chrissy Bristow – Beadwork Tutor
1 Highbury Villas, Ash Green Road, Ash Green, Surrey GU12 6JF
t 01252 312326
e chrissy.bristow@virgin.net
w www.chrissybristow.co.uk
Chrissy teaches off-loom beadwork and bead crochet. Also accepts commissions. See also Private Colleges and Workshop Organisers (Creative Needles); Textile Artists and Designers.

Charisma Beads
25 Churchyard, Hitchin, Herts SG5 1HP
t 01462 454054
e sales@charismabeads.co.uk
w www.charismabeads.co.uk
Your one-stop beadwork shop! Retail and mail order.

Melanie de Miguel
126 St Georges Drive, Watford, Herts WD19 5HD
t 07740 853999 f 020 8386 8348
e beadymelonwheels@yahoo.co.uk
One-day workshops to learn traditional/modern, hand and loom techniques to create jewellery, 3-D structures, wirework and artefacts. See ad on p. 20.

(The) Earring Café
53b Mount Street, Coventry CV5 8DE
t 024 7671 4501 f 024 7671 4501
e amanda@earringcafe.co.uk
w www.earringcafe.co.uk
Glass beadmaker, making unique collectors' beads, big and small. Buy online, by mail order or ask for my list of fairs.

Fabrics for Fun/Beads for Beauty
32 Babbacombe Road, Torquay TQ1 3SN
t 01803 328902 f 01803 328902
e charles@wraymcann.freeserve.co.uk
Good variety of seed, cube and bugle beads. Nymo, jewellery and craft wires, looms. Beading kits. Workshop programme. 4 x 27p stamps please. See also Mail Order Suppliers (Fabrics).

Sylvia Fairhurst - Beadwork Tutor 🅣
11 Randolph Close, Bradville, Milton Keynes
MK13 7JN
t 01908 311243 f 01908 579341
e witch.beads@btclick.com
w www.witchbeads.com
Tuition of beadwork, basic techniques and beyond.
Workshops, talks and demonstrations. Mail order
beads and original designs in kit form.

Fine Lines 🅣
17 Broad Street, Seaford, East Sussex BN25 1LS
t 01323 891152
e kjwilliams@eurobell.co.uk
w www.delica-beads.co.uk
The south coast's specialist bead shop, selling every-
thing beady you'll ever needy!! Delicas in over 500
colours. Travelling shop/tutor. See ad on p. 16.

Lynn Firth 🅣
9 The Limes, Motcombe, Dorset SP7 9QL
t 01747 855076 f 01747 850751
e lynnfirth@stitchncraft.co.uk
w www.stitchncraft.co.uk
Wide variety of beadwork workshops beginners to
advanced including freeform, 3D flowers and
more. Please enquire for up-to-date workshop list.

GJ Beads 🅣
Unit 1, Court Arcade, The Wharf, St Ives,
Cornwall TR26 1LG
t 01736 793886 f 01736 793886
e beadyspice@aol.com
w www.gjbeads.co.uk
Visit our website to view/buy from a wide
selection of beading books and seed beads or
email us with any other requirements.
See ad on p. 20.

Glass Beadmakers UK
Middle House, 34 Grecian Street, Aylesbury
HP20 1LT
t 01296 437406
e mail@gbuk.fsworld.co.uk
w www.gbuk.fsworld.co.uk
Fantastic contemporary glass beads by UK
makers. Join us to learn glass beadmaking or
drool and buy!

Halfpenney's Coffee Shop & Embroidery Centre 🅣
The Old Toll House, 1-5 Parson Lane,
Clitheroe, Lancs BB7 2JP
t 01200 424478 f 01200 424478
e g&t@halfpenney.ndo.co.uk
w www.halfpenney.ndo.co.uk
Evening classes are held regularly in our
delightful coffee and embroidery shop.
Embroidery and beadweaving supplies.

Gillian Lamb - Bead Teacher 🅣
16 Firwood Close, St Johns, Woking GU21 1UQ
t 01483 476356
e gillian.lamb@ntlworld.com
Fun bead classes for all levels and abilities.

London Bead Co./Delicate Stitches 🅣
339 Kentish Town Road, London NW5 2TJ
t 0870 203 2323 f 0207 284 2062
e lonbeads@dialstart.net
2000 square feet Aladdin's Cave, directly o
pposite tube station. Bead and embroidery
products galore. Classes available all year round.

Jill Nicholls 🅣
Pen Cwmrhaffau, Sarnau, Llandysul,
Ceredigion SA44 6QZ
t 01239 811288
e jill@techstyle.org.uk
Jill Nicholls is an experienced textile and
beadwork artist and teacher. She specialises in
creative off-loom techniques.

Rosarama Beadcraft 🅣
2 Beech Grove Terrace, Crawcrook, Ryton,
Gateshead, Tyne and Wear NE40 4LZ
t 0191 413 9111 f 0191 413 9111
e rosarama@btinternet.com
Beads, in many shapes, sizes and colours,
findings, embroidery and sewing threads, card-
making materials and more. Workshops available.
£3 mail order catalogue.

Libby Smith 🅣
11 Philips Close, Rayne, Nr Braintree, Essex
CM77 6DB
t 01376 325765 f 01376 325765
e libby.smith@tesco.net
Workshops on beaded tassels, incorporating a
variety of materials including metal threads,
cords, fabrics, gimps, glitter, moulds and
embroidery threads.

Stitch 'n' Craft 🅣

Swan's Yard Craft Centre, High Street, Shaftesbury, Dorset SP7 8JQ

t 01747 852500 **f** 01747 850751

e enquiries@stitchncraft.co.uk

w www.stitchncraft.co.uk

A wide range of craft, embroidery and beading supplies together with an exciting and varied workshop programme. Mail order service available. See ad on p. 38.

Liz Thornton 🅣

4 Honor Oak Road, Forest Hill, London SE23 3SF

t 0208 291 5029

e eathornton@btinternet.com

Beadwork tutor - beginners to advanced - all major techniques. Local authority-run classes in London. Willing to travel to groups and guilds.

Pat Trott - Beadwork Tutor 🅣

82 Halstead Walk, Allington, Maidstone, Kent ME16 0PW

t 01622 750910

Passionate about beads, I teach needle bead weaving, beaded crochet and knitting and even how to make your own beautiful millefiore. See also Textile Artists and Designers

Sandra Wallace 🅣

3 Ivy Bank, Yeadon, Nr Leeds LS19 7HJ

t 0113 250 7396

C&G classes in Beadweaving. Talks and workshops in many beadweaving techniques. Special interest in Native American beadwork. See also Textile Artists and Designers.

West of England Bead Fair 🅣

c/o Swan's Yard Craft Centre, High Street, Shaftesbury, Dorset SP7 8JQ

t 01747 852500 **f** 01747 850751

e lynnfirth@stitchncraft.co.uk

w westofenglandbeadfair.co.uk

15 June 2003 at Wincanton Racecourse. Workshops, trade stands, exhibitions, demonstrations and refreshments. (See also Conferences/Major Events/Shows; ad on p.38.)

World Embroidery 🅣

2 Woodlands, Kirby Misperton, Malton, North Yorkshire YO17 6XW

t 01653 697254

e worldembroidery@kirbymisperton.freeserve.co.uk

Beads, bells, shells and shisha. Beading and embroidery classes. See also Foreign Textile Studies; Mail Order Suppliers (Embroidery).

Fanny Wright 🅣

The Trumpet, West End, Minchinhampton, Gloucestershire GL6 9JA

t 01453 883027

e antiques@thetrumpet.free-online.co.uk

Sculptural/free beaded jewellery, including traditional techniques. Create a beautiful sculptural piece and turn it into earrings, bracelet or necklace.

Yellow Brick Road 🅣

8 Bachelors Walk, Dublin 1, Ireland

t + 353 1 8730177 **f** + 353 1 8730177

e stacey@yellowbrickroad.ie

w www.yellowbrickroad.ie

Premium quality beads and findings. Jewellery-making courses from September to May. Beadweaving tuition also available. Holder of City & Guilds Certificate.

Bead shops and tutors by area

East Anglia	South Central	South West	Ireland
Libby Smith	Beady Babas	Fabrics for Fun/Beads for Beauty	Yellow Brick Road
Midlands	**South East**	Lynn Firth	
Sylvia Fairhurst	Chrissy Bristow	GJ Beads	
Fanny Wright	Charisma Beads	Stitch 'n' Craft	
North East	Melanie de Miguel	West of England Bead Fair	
Rosarama Beadcraft	Fine Lines		**Wales**
Sandra Wallace	Gillian Lamb		Jill Nicholls
World Embroidery	London Bead Co.		
North West	Liz Thornton		
21st Century Beads	Pat Trott		

Booksellers

Avril Whittle Bookseller
Whittle's Warehouse, 7-9 (Rear) Bainbridge Road, Sedbergh, Cumbria LA10 5AU
t 01539 621770 f 01539 621770
e avrilsbooks@aol.com
Scarce books on all aspects of the textile arts. Search service. Stock printouts by subject. Enquiries welcomed. Visitors by appointment.

Black Cat Books
Meadow Cottage, High Road, Worwell, Harleston, Norfolk IP20 0EN
t 01986 788826 f 01986 788826
e ann@blackcatbooks.co.uk
w blackcatbooks.co.uk
Costume & fashion, textiles & design, needlework & lace. Est. 1984. Visitors welcome (telephone first). Can sometimes deliver books to shows.

Bowdon Books
33 Lowergate, Clitheroe, Lancashire BB7 1AD
t 01200 425333 f 01200 443490
e gor15@dial.pipex.com
w ukbookworld.com/members/bowdonbooks
Buying and selling books on textile arts. Shop, internet, book fairs and postal business. Gallery featuring rarely seen textile artists.

Felicity J Warnes Bookseller
The Old Bookshop, 36 Gordon Road, Enfield, Middlesex EN2 0PZ
t 020 8367 1661
f 020 8372 1035
e felicity@fjwarnes.u-net.com
w www.fjwarnes.u-net.com
Secondhand and out-of-print books on costume, fashion, lace, textiles, embroidery. Shop open by appointment only.

Four Shire Bookshop
17 High Street, Moreton-in-Marsh, Gloucestershire GL56 0AF
t 01608 651451 f 01608 651451
e fourshirebooks@aol.com
Books on design and quilting, patchwork, embroidery, crochet, knitting, needlework. New and old. Booksearch service.

John Ives Bookseller
5 Normanhurst Drive, Twickenham, Middlesex TW1 1NA
t 020 8892 6265 f 020 8744 3944
e jives@btconnect.com
Books on textiles (including out-of-print titles). Worldwide mail order. Ask for latest catalogue.

Judith Mansfield Books
Claremont South, Burnley Road, Todmorden, Lancs OL14 5LH
t 01706 816487 f 01706 816487
e todmordenbooks@ndirect.co.uk
Antiquarian and secondhand books on textile arts bought and sold. Regular catalogues issued. Visits by appointment. See ad on p. 30.

Keith Smith Books
78b The Homend, Ledbury, Herefordshire HR8 1BX
t 01531 635336 f 0870 0529986
e sallyferriday@ksbooks.demon.co.uk
Secondhand and out-of-print books on textiles and needlecrafts. Shop open Monday-Saturday 10-5. Regular catalogues. See ad on p. 20.

Well Head Books
The Old Vicarage, Bourton, Gillingham, Dorset SP8 5BJ
t 01747 840213 f 01747 840724
e wellheadbooks@aol.com
Specialist textile and beading bookseller. Mail order and shows only.

Booksellers listed by area

East Anglia
Black Cat Books

Midlands
Four Shire Bookshop
Keith Smith Books

North West
Avril Whittle Bookseller
Bowdon Books
Judith Mansfield Books

South East
Felicity J Warnes Bookseller
John Ives Bookseller

South West
Well Head Books

Conferences/Major Events/Shows

Art in Action
96 Sedlescombe Road, London SW6 1RB
t 020 7381 3192 **f** 020 7381 0605
e info@artinaction.org.uk
w www.artinaction.org.uk
Art festival where over 300 artists and craftsmen work before the public. 17-20 July 2003, Waterperry House, Nr Wheatley, Oxford.

Grosvenor Exhibitions Ltd
21 High Street, Spalding, Lincs PE11 1TX
t 01775 712100 **f** 01775 713125
e house@gxu.co.uk
w www.grosvenor-publishing.co.uk
Organisers of the National Quilt Championships (Sandown Park) 26-29 June, Quilts UK (Malvern) 15-18 May, The Great Northern Quilt Festival (Harrogate) 18-21 September.

HALI Antique Carpet and Textile Art Fair
St Giles House, 50 Poland Street, London W1F 7FN
t 020 7970 4600 **f** 020 7578 7221
e farzins@centaur.co.uk
The world's premier antique carpet and textile art fair showcasing woven artifacts from 90 dealers and 20 countries.

ICHF (International Craft & Hobby Fair Ltd)
Dominic House, Seaton Road, Highcliffe, Dorset BH23 5HW
t 01425 272711 **f** 01425 279369
e info@ichf.co.uk
w www.ichf.co.uk
UK's No 1 creative crafts and gift show organiser. A feast of displays, supplies, demonstrations, talks and workshops.

John & Jennifer Ford/The National Christmas Lacemaker's Fair
October Hill, Upper Longdon, Rugeley, Staffordshire WS15 1QB
t 01543 491000
e j.ford@lace-making.com
w www.lace-making.com
Christmas Lacemaker's Fair at NEC Birmingham. 30 November and 1 December 2002. Over 100 exhibitors. Details telephone number above or website.

(The) Knitting and Stitching Shows
Creative Exhibitions, 8 Greenwich Quay, Clarence Road, London SE8 3EY
t 020 8692 2299 **f** 020 8692 6699
e mail@twistedthread.com
w www.twistedthread.com
The definitive textiles event in the UK; excellent shopping for the enthusiast and great inspiration for the non-stitcher!

Maria Peters Quilters Days
Vourden, Cracknore Hard Lane, Marchwood, Hampshire SO40 4UT
t 023 8086 2843
e petersvourden@talk21.com
Speakers Cathy Hoover (USA), Annette Morgan (UK) plus shoppers mall, quilt show/competition and workshops by the speakers.

Nationwide Exhibitions
PO Box 20, Fishponds, Bristol BS16 5QU
t 0117 907 1000 **f** 0117 907 1001
e user@nwe.co.uk
w www.nwe.co.uk
Organisers of well-established, very successful Knit, Stitch & Creative Craft Shows. Locations - Surrey, Manchester, Belfast, Somerset, Birmingham and Edinburgh.

Quilts, Inc
7660 Woodway, Suite 550, Houston, Texas 77063, USA
t +1 713 781 6864 **f** +1 713 781 8182
e shows@quilts.com
w www.quilts.com
Consumer shows of patchwork & quilting with vendors, classes and special exhibits. Festivals - Oct/Nov 02 in Houston, April 03 in Rosemont, IL (near Chicago).

Rootie Tootie Designs
291 Eldon St, Greenock, Renfrewshire PA16 7QL
t 01475 659315
e rklamont22@yahoo.co.uk
Designs and ideas for installations and all types of art work creating themes and images for all your marketing requirements. See also Textile Artists and Designers (Ruth Kathryn Lamont).

West of England Bead Fair

c/o Swan's Yard Craft Centre, High Street,
Shaftesbury, Dorset SP7 8JQ
e 01747 852500 f 01747 850751
e lynnfirth@stitchncraft.co.uk
w westofenglandbeadfair.co.uk
15 June 2003 at Wincanton Racecourse.
Workshops, trade stands, exhibitions,
demonstrations and refreshments. See also
Beads, Beads, Beads.

www.quiltfest.com

Mancuso Inc., Dept TD, PO Box 667, New
Hope, PA 18938, USA
t +1 215 862 5828 f +1 215 862 9753
e mancuso@quiltfest.com
w www.quiltfest.com
Mancuso Show Management presents 6 major
quilting and textile art events each year.
See ad on p. 42.

Days Out and Fun for All

(The) Earnley Concourse 🅣

Earnley, Chichester, West Sussex PO20 7JL
t 01243 670392 f 01243 670832
e info@earnley.co.uk
w www.earnley.co.uk
Residential leisure interest courses for adults.
Textile subjects include embroidery, silk
painting/batik, patchwork, rag rugging, tapestry
weaving and handspinning.

Orkney Angora

Isle of Sanday, Orkney KW17 2AZ,
Scotland
t 01857 600421
e info@orkneyangora.co.uk
w www.orkneyangora.co.uk
Specialist producer of angora thermal clothing
and accessories. Extensive colourful range
including underwear. Rabbits can usually
be seen.

Quarry Bank Mill 🅣

Styal, Cheshire SK9 4LA
t 01625 527468 f 01625 539267
e quarrybankmill@ntrust.org.uk
w www.quarrybankmill.org.uk
Textile-based activities, adult and children's
workshops in historic working cotton mill set in
beautiful National Trust Styal Estate.

Sulgrave Manor 🅣

Manor Road, Sulgrave, Banbury, Oxon
OX17 2SD
t 01295 760205 f 01925 768056
e sulgrave-manor@talk21.com
w www.stratford.co.uk/sulgrave
Tudor manor house offering needlework-biased
guided tours for pre-booked groups plus
needlework events throughout the year.

Texere Yarns

College Mill, Barkerend Road, Bradford
BD1 4AU
t 0871 717 1129 f 0871 717 1139
e enquiries @texereyarns.co.uk
w www.texereyarns.co.uk
An exciting collection of yarns for creative textile
arts and crafts, available by mail order or from
the mill shop.

Whitchurch Silk Mill 🅣

28 Winchester Street, Whitchurch,
Hampshire RG28 7AL
t 01256 892065
e silkmill@btinternet.com
w whitchurchsilkmill.org.uk
Heritage watermill with working Victorian silk
weaving machinery. Kids' holiday activities,
adult workshops, school programmes. Shop,
tearoom, phone for opening times.

23

Diary Dates – Major Shows

JANUARY
16-19 Knit, Stitch & Creative Crafts Show, Sandown Park Exhibition Centre

FEBRUARY
7-9 Creative Stitches & Hobbycrafts, Brighton
14-16 Spring Quilt Festival, Ardingley

FEBRUARY/MARCH
28-2 Spring Quilt Festival, Edinburgh

MARCH
6-9 Creative Stitches & Hobbycrafts, SECC, Glasgow
14-16 Knit, Stitch & Creative Crafts Show, G-MEX Centre, Manchester
20-23 Sewing for Pleasure & Hobbycrafts, NEC, Birmingham

21-23, Spring Quilt Festival, Chilford Hall, Cambridge

APRIL
10-12 Knit, Stitch & Creative Crafts Show, Kings Hall, Belfast
24-27 Knit, Stitch & Creative Crafts Show, Bath & West Showground, Shepton Mallet

MAY
8-11 The Great British Bead Show, Daventry
15-18 Quilts UK, Malvern

JUNE
5-8 The HALI Antique Textile and Carpet Fair, Olympia
15 West of England Bead Fair, Wincanton Racecourse
26-29 National Quilt Championships, Sandown Park

JULY
13 Bead Fair, Dorking

SEPTEMBER
18-21 Great Northern Quilt Show, Harrogate

OCTOBER
9-12 The Knitting and Stitching Show, Alexandra Palace

OCTOBER/NOVEMBER
30-2 The Knitting and Stitching Show, Dublin

NOVEMBER
7-9 Autumn Quilt Fair, Chilford Hall, Cambridge
20-23 The Knitting and Stitching Show, Harrogate

24

Distance Learning

(The) Crafty Computer
Old Mill House, The Causeway, Hitcham,
Suffolk IP7 7NF
t 01449 741747 f 01449 740118
e creatively42@aol.com
w www.muntus.co.uk
*On-line magazine offering help, tutorials, short
and longer courses, and advice on computers,
design programs and image manipulation for the
textile enthusiast. See ad on p. 24.*

Crochet Design
17 Poulton Square, Morecambe, Lancs LA4 5PZ
t 01524 831752 f 01524 833099
e paulineturner@crochet.co.uk
w www.crochet.co.uk
*High standard Diploma in Crochet is in three
parts - Techniques; Commercial Designing;
Mixed Media Artforms - and recognised
internationally.*

Eccles Farm School of Stitched Textiles
Eccles Farm Needlecraft Centre, Eccles Lane,
Bispham Green, Ormskirk, Lancashire L40 3SD
t 01257 463163/463113
e enquiries@schoolofstitchedtextiles.com
w www.schoolofstitchedtextiles.com
*City & Guilds Embroidery and Patchwork
courses. Workshops at the farm and retail sales
for patchwork and creative embroidery.*

are you not listed or have you
spotted someone else missing?

your contributions are vital to the
growth of the textile directory

you can fill in the form on our
website, email, fax, phone or snail
mail us a line

w www.thetextiledirectory.com
e list@thetextiledirectory.com
t 0870 220 2423 f 01386 760401
The Textile Directory, Word4Word,
107 High Street, Evesham WR11 4EB

Kersbrook Training
2 Kersbrook Cross, Bray Shop, Callington,
Cornwall PL17 8QW
t 01566 782907 f 01566 782907
e pfsatkersbrook@cornwall-county.com
w www.kersbrooktraining.co.uk
*Mixed textiles, embroidery, tapestry weaving,
feltmaking, handknitting, machine embroidery,
fabric decoration. Above all FUN. Accredited
City & Guilds centre. See ad on p. 24.*

Open College of the Arts
Unit 1B, Redbrook Business Park, Wilthorpe
Road, Barnsley S75 1JN
t 01226 730495 f 01226 730838
e open.arts@ukonline.co.uk
w www.oca-uk.com
*Design textiles in a personal and creative way on
one of our long-established courses with expert
tutorial support.*

Opus School of Textile Arts
20 Crown Street, Harrow on the Hill,
Middlesex HA2 0HR
t 020 8864 7283 f 020 8423 3001
e enquiries@opus-online.co.uk
w www.opus-online.co.uk
*Creative embroidery and textile courses from
beginners to degree level that can be studied from
anywhere in the world. See also Higher
Education/Research Centres; Private Colleges
and Workshop Organisers; ad on p. 54.*

Patchwork Post
5 Kingswood Road, Dunton Green,
Sevenoaks, Kent TN13 2XE
t 01732 462653 f 01732 462653
*Parts 1 & 2 C&G Patchwork & Quilting.
Professional tuition. Study at your leisure.
Enrolment throughout the year.*

WS Touchbase
Main Street, Broadmayne, Dorchester DT2 8EB
t 01305 854099 f 01305 854099
e admin@wstouchbase.co.uk
w wstouchbase.co.uk
*Come and 'touchbase' for City & Guilds textile
courses in distance learning format. Professional
tutors for learning with distinction!*

Exhibiting Groups

62 Group of Textile Artists
PO Box 24615, London E2 7TU
w www.62group.freeuk.com
International, professional exhibiting group

Alive and Stitching
c/o Jo Owen, 12 Bents Green Avenue,
Sheffield S11 7RB
t 0114 230 3030
e joowen10@hotmail.com
w www.aliveandstitching.co.uk
*Six professional textile artists, producing
exhibitions of highly original work, diverse in
colour, form, content and size.*

Forthcoming exhibition at Treeline, Diamond Court,
Bakewell, 1 Nov - 7 Dec 2002, t 01629 813749

EAST ⓣ
46 Spring Way, Sible Hedingham, Halstead,
Essex CO9 3SB
t 01787 469363 f 01787 469362
e c.a.dixon@talk21.com
*Exciting, challenging, innovative group of artists
based in East Anglia. Meet regularly, exhibit,
work to commission, give workshops & talks.*

'Take Eleven plus One', The Manor House Museum, 18
Dec 2002 - 31 Jan2003, one-day open workshop 18 Jan
2003; Art Van Go (see Art Galleries), 17-26 April 2003

(The) Fiber Connection ⓣ
1064 Lake Placid Dr, Toms River, NJ 08753, USA
*An award-winning international group of quilt
and textile artists.*

Fibre Art Wales ⓣ
Penwmrhaffau, Sarnau, Llandysul,
Ceredigion SA44 6QZ
t 01239 811288
e jill@techstyle.org.uk
w www.fibreartwales.freeuk.com
*The group aim to promote both their own work and
stimulate interest in this area of the visual arts.*

'Fibre Visions, Bangor Museum & Art Gallery,
Gwynned, Jan-Mar 2003

Fibreworks
14 West Hill, Hitchin, Herts SG5 2HZ
t 01462 454823 f 01462 434295
e barry.arends@ivories.demon.co.uk
*An established group of designer-makers whose
aim is to explore the medium of constructed
textiles as an art form.*

Images in Stitch
50 Hillside Gardens, Barnet, Herts EN5 2NJ
t 020 8441 1128
e imagesinstitch@aol.com
w www.imagesinstitch.co.uk
*Textile artists from SW Herts. Individual
members teach, lecture, write, make vestments,
repair textiles and embroider for couture.
Commissions welcome.*

New Embroidery Group
c/o 105 Dulwich Village, London SE21 7BJ
t 020 8693 3740
e annrutherford@onetel.net.uk
w www.newembroiderygroup.co.uk
*Countrywide membership. Open to professional and
amateur textile artists. Meetings and visits. Design
courses. Regular exhibitions of selected work.*

(The) South London Textile Workshop ⓣ
c/o Lindsey Green, Secretary, 35 Somerville
Road, Penge, London SE20 7NA
t 020 8659 6997
e Lindsey.Green@oyeznet.co.uk
*The group meets fortnightly and works in a
variety of textile techniques, including weaving,
feltmaking, embroidery, knitting and beading.*

Studio 21 ⓣ
c/o The Coach House, Ridgeway Road,
Dorking, Surrey RH4 3EY
t 01306 883057
*Studio 21 is an exhibiting group formed in 1997
who create innovative contemporary stitched
textiles. We do commissions and take workshops.*

Exhibitions of work
Guildford House, Guildford High Street, May 2003
Upfront Gallery, Caldbeck, Cumbria, Sept/Oct 2003

Visions Group of Textile Artists
2 Oak Way, Frisby on the Wreake, Melton
Mowbray, Leicestershire LE14 2NF
t 01664 434349
e annesmedley@onetel.net.uk
w http://freespace.virgin.net/pritchardfamily/visions
*Visions exhibits and sells contemporary textile art
and embroidery, members individually producing
a diversity of exciting and innovative work.*

Foreign Textile Studies

China International Academy for Weaving and Embroidery

c/o Turid Uthaug, Danish Weaving Centre, Fjelstrup 34, 6100 Haderslev, Denmark
t +45 7452 7675 **f** +45 7453 4222
e wcenter@mail.danbbs.dk
w www.weaving-center.dk
Courses in traditional Chinese weaving and embroidery. For beginners and advanced students. Peace: Suzhou, China. Chinese teachers. Instruction in English.

Danish Weaving Centre

Fjelstrup 34, 6100 Haderslev, Denmark
t +45 7452 7675 **f** +45 7453 4222
e wcenter@mail.danbbs.dk
w www.weaving-center.dk
Weaving courses for beginners as well as advanced weavers. Glimaalcra looms. Instruction languages: Scandinavian languages, English and German.

Japanese Embroidery Guild

53 Maresfield Gardens, London NW3 5TE
t 020 7794 7250
Exquisite traditional designs, superb silks, glorious golds. Tuition and advice on traditional Japanese embroidery techniques throughout the UK.

Japanese Embroidery UK - The Nuido Group

PO Box 815, Knaphill, Woking, Surrey GU21 2WH
t 01483 476246 **f** 01483 836152
e info@japaneseembroideryuk.com
w www.japaneseembroideryuk.com
Tuition in history/techniques of traditional Japanese embroidery/stitched beading. Classes or one-to-one with authorised UK tutors. S.a.e. for information.

Claire Weldon

78-80 Troutbeck, Albany Street, London NW1 4EJ
t 07373 432006 **f** 020 7388 8815
e claireweldon@ambika.co.uk
I give slide talks on Nakshe kantha embroidery from Bangladesh with hands-on examples. Kantha pieces and books available to buy.

World Embroidery

2 Woodlands, Kirby Misperton, Malton, North Yorkshire YO17 6XW
t 01653 697254
e worldembroidery@kirbymisperton.freeserve.co.uk
Workshops and talks, and textile collection to visit (by arrangement). Textiles from North West and Central India and Central Asia. See also Beads, Beads, Beads; Mail Order Suppliers (Embroidery).

This is a new section in the Directory. Please let us know if you know of anyone else that specialises in the teaching or studying of foreign textiles

Moderna Jat girl from Banni in Kutch India, kindly provided by Lorna Tresidder of Indian Romance, see Textile Tours, p. 108.

Higher Education/Research Centres

Bishop Burton College
Bishop Burton, Beverley, East Yorkshire
HU17 8QG
t 01964 553000 f 01964 553101
e enquiries@bishopburton.ac.uk
w www.bishopburton.ac.uk
*HNC Textiles (part-time), HND Textiles
(full-time). Highly qualified staff, exciting
innovative work.*

Central Saint Martins College of Art &
Design, School of Fashion & Textile
Design
109 Charing Cross Road, London WC2H 0DU
t 020 7514 7000 f 020 7514 7152
e applications@csm.linst.ac.uk
w www.csm.linst.ac.uk
*Degree courses, postgraduate courses
and research in textile design for interiors
and/or fashion.*

Cleveland College of Art & Design
Church Square, Hartlepool, Cleveland
TS24 7EX
t 01429 422000 f 01429 422122
e tricia.mckenzie@ccad.ac.uk
w www.ccad.ac.uk
*BA (Hons) Textiles and Surface Design (full-
time and part-time) enables students to develop
skills in printed textiles, embroidery, surface
design and manipulation.*

Cumbria Institute of the Arts
Brampton Road, Carlisle, Cumbria CA3 9AY
t 01228 400300 f 01228 514491
e q@cumbria.ac.uk
w www.cumbria.ac.uk
*Specialist textile resources in embroidered,
printed and constructed textiles, including
CAD/CAM facilities and specialist rug-tufting
and millinery equipment.*

Glasgow School of Art
167 Renfrew Street, Glasgow G3 6RQ
t 0141 353 4626 f 0141 353 4745
e l.taylor@gsa.ac.uk
w www.gsa.ac.uk
*BA (Hons) Design - Textiles, encompassing
weave, print, knit, embroidery. Research centre
for digitally printed textiles, education, research
and commercial service.*

Goldsmiths College
New Cross, London E14 6NW
t 020 7919 7671 f 020 7919 7673
e visual-arts@gold.ac.uk
w www.goldsmiths.ac.uk
*The College pursues excellence in visual, literary
and performing arts, social, behavioural and
mathematical sciences, design, humanities and
educational studies.*

Heriot-Watt University, School of Textiles
and Design
Netherdale, Galashiels, Selkirkshire TD1 3HF
t 01896 753351 f 01896 758965
e enquiries@hw.ac.uk
w www.hw.ac.uk
*Undergraduate and postgraduate courses in
textile design, fashion, clothing and technology.
Postgraduate research in these areas.*

Jewel and Esk Valley College, Creative
Industries and Arts
24 Milton Road East, Edinburgh EH15 2PP
t 0131 660 1010 f 0131 657 2276
e info@jevc.ac.uk
w www.jevc.ac.uk
*City & Guilds courses in Patchwork/Quilting,
Embroidery, Machine Embroidery & Fashion.
Creative textiles for today. Individual tuition &
support.*

London Guildhall University
41 Commercial Road, London E1 1LA
t 020 7320 1880/1853
e ashbrook@lgu.ac.uk
*BA Textile Furnishing Design and Manufacture
- specialising in the design of 3D textile artifacts,
engaging cultural, practical and technological
standpoints.*

Loughborough University School of Art &
Design
Epinal Way, Loughborough, Leicestershire
LE11 3TU
t 01509 228936 f 01509 228902
e d.johnson@lboro.ac.uk
w www.lboro.ac.uk
*BA (Hons) courses in printed textiles,
woven textiles and multi-media textiles. Pre-
degree foundation courses. Post-graduate
MPhil research.*

Opus School of Textile Arts

20 Crown Street, Harrow on the Hill,
Middlesex HA2 0HR
t 020 8864 7283 **f** 020 8423 3001
e enquiries@opus-online.co.uk
w www.opus-online.co.uk
Opus offers the first BA (Hons) Embroidered Textiles by distance learning, validated by Middlesex University. Creative embroidery and textile courses from beginners to degree level that can be studied from anywhere in the world. See also Distance Learning; Private Colleges and Workshop Organisers; ad on p. 54.

(The) Surrey Institute of Art & Design, University College

Falkner Road, Farnham, Surrey GU9 7DS
t 01252 722441 **f** 01252 892616
e registry@surrart.ac.uk
Three-year full-time BA (Hons) degree programme in Textiles: Printed and Woven. Also home to the Crafts Study Centre and the new Anglo-Japanese Textile Research Centre.

University of Central England in Birmingham

BIAD, Corporation Street, Birmingham
B4 7DX
t 0121 331 5820 **f** 0121 331 5821
e joanne.binks@uce.ac.uk
w www.biad.uce.ac.uk
The BA (Hons) Textile Design course offers specialisms in constructed textiles, embroidery or printed textiles with a retail management option.

University of Huddersfield, Department of Textiles

Queensgate, Huddersfield HD1 3DH
t 01484 442653 **f** 01484 472826
e p.l.squires@hud.ac.uk
BA (Hons) Creative Textile Crafts course provides a stimulating environment in which to develop aesthetic, intellectual and multimedia textile crafts skills.

University of Leeds School of Textiles and Design

University of Leeds, Leeds LS2 9JT
t 0113 343 3700 **f** 0113 343 3704
e j.e.mitchell@leeds.ac.uk **w** www.leeds.ac.uk
Undergraduate and postgraduate programmes of study in textiles and fashion, design, management, retailing and technology.

West Dean College

Chichester, West Sussex PO18 0QZ
t 01243 811301 **f** 01243 811343
e enquiries@westdean.org.uk
w www.westdean.org.uk
Short courses in textile media (embroidery, stitch, painting, printing, dyeing, weaving, lace-making and other techniques). Postgraduate diplomas in tapestry weaving. See also Adult and Further Education; Private Colleges and Workshop Organisers; Textile Artists and Designers.

Winchester School of Art

Faculty of Arts, University of Southampton, Highfield, Southampton, Hampshire SO17 1BF
t 023 8059 6718 **f** 023 8059 5437
e artsrec@soton.ac.uk
w www.wsa.soton.ac.uk
We offer a wide range of fashion, textile art and textile design courses at foundation, undergraduate and postgraduate levels.

Higher Education by area

Midlands
Loughborough University
University of Central England in Birmingham

North East
Bishop Burton College
Cleveland College
University of Leeds

North West
Cumbria Institute of the Arts
University of Huddersfield

Scotland
Glasgow School of Art
Heriot-Watt University
Jewel and Esk Valley College

South Central
West Dean College

South East
Central Saint Martins College of Art & Design
Goldsmiths College
London Guildhall University
Opus School of Textile Arts
Surrey Institute of Art & Design
Winchester School of Art

Mail Order Suppliers

Art Materials

Ario 🔴
5 Pengry Road, Loughor, Swansea SA4 6PH
t 01792 529092/01792 429849 **f** 01792 529092
e fiona@ario.co.uk **w** www.ario.co.uk
See us for papers, fabrics, books, lazertran, wiremesh, Stewart Gill, Brusho, inks, dyes, lustre powders, textured gels. Workshops by arrangement.

Art Van Go 🔴
The Studios, 1 Stevenage Road, Knebworth, Hertfordshire SG3 6AN
t 01438 814946 **f** 01438 816267
e art@artvango.co.uk **w** www.artvango.co.uk
Art materials, etc. for fine art and textile artists by mail order and mobile shop. Workshops for groups at their venue. See also Art Galleries and Exhibitions; Mail Order Suppliers (Dyes/Silk Paints); Shops (Art Materials; Dyes/Silk Paints); Private Colleges and Workshop Organisers; ad on inside front cover.

Bags of Inspiration 🔴
4 Sunningdale Road, Wallasey, Wirral CH45 0LU
e boinsp@yahoo.com
Supply textiles and art goods to C&G students, foundation and textile artists, visit colleges, universities and groups. Education orders taken.

Dorset Decoupage 🔴
21 Penn Hill Avenue, Parkstone, Poole, Dorset BH14 9LU
t 01202 778321
3D découpage materials. Videos and tuition. Send £4.50 for catalogue.

George Weil with Fibrecrafts
Old Portsmouth Road, Peasmarsh, Guildford, Surrey GU3 1LZ
t 01483 565800 **f** 01483 565807
e sales@georgeweil.co.uk
w www.georgeweil.co.uk
Suppliers of materials and equipment for colour and dyeing, surface decoration, fibre crafts and yarn crafts with next day delivery.

Lazertran Ltd
8 Alban Square, Aberaeron, Ceredigion SA46 0AD
t 01545 571149 **f** 01545 571187
e si@lazertran.com
w www.lazertran.com
Lazertran transfer papers add a new dimension to many aspects of textile art. See ad on p. 35.

(The) Paper Shed 🔴
March House, Tollerton, York YO61 1QQ
t 01347 838253 **f** 01347 838096
e papershed@papershed.com
w www.papershed.com
Handmade papers, papermaking equipment, pulps; silk fibres, papers and kits; a cornucopia of textures for the textile artist.

Buttons, etc.

(The) Button Lady
16 Hollyfield Road South, Sutton Coldfield, West Midlands B76 1NX
t 0121 329 3234
Buttons and clasps in natural materials, large range of shapes in various materials, charms, Cash's labels and address labels.

Gregory Knopp
PO Box 158, Gillingham, Kent ME7 3HF
t 01634 375706 **f** 01634 263155
e info@gregory-knopp.co.uk
w www.gregory-knopp.co.uk
Over 300 different embellishments and buttons
for all textile crafts. Suppliers of thread racks,
Able stretchers and quilting stands.

L Nichols Vintage Handmade
Glass Buttons
35 Addington Square, London SE5 7LB
t 020 7701 3433
e nicbutns@lineone.net
w www.nicholsbuttons.co.uk
L Nichols handmade glass buttons for the Fifties
couture houses. Wonderful buttons found from
his stock for any project.

Talisman Buttons
29 Coutts Avenue, Shorne, Gravesend,
Kent DA12 3HJ
t 01474 822960
We have possibly the largest selection of buttons
in the UK, including novelty, children's, wooden,
natural shell, etc.

Conservation Materials

Restore Products
2 Talbot Road, Bowdon, Altrincham,
Cheshire WA14 3JD
t 0161 928 0020 **f** 0161 928 0020
e products@textilerestoration.co.uk
w www.textilerestoration.co.uk
Specialist conservation materials, including fine
threads and curved needles, acid-free tissue and
storage boxes, detergent and iron mould remover.

Dyes/Silk Paints

Art Van Go
The Studios, 1 Stevenage Road, Knebworth,
Hertfordshire SG3 6AN
t 01438 814946 **f** 01438 816267
e art@artvango.co.uk **w** www.artvango.co.uk
Dyes, fabrics and accessories for the silk painter
and textile artist by mail order and mobile shop.
See also Art Galleries and Exhibitions; Mail
Order Suppliers (Art Materials); Private
Colleges and Workshop Organisers; Shops
(Art Materials; Dyes/Silk Paints); ad on inside
front cover.

Colourcraft Colours & Adhesives Ltd
Unit 5, 555 Carlisle Street East, Sheffield S4 8DT
t 0114 242 1431 **f** 0114 243 4844
e colourcraftltd@aol.com
w www.colourcraftltd.com
UK manufacturers and distributors of an
extensive range of quality fabric dyes, paints,
printing systems and auxilary chemicals.

Dye-Namik Craft Supplies
3 Canal Cottages, Hanbury Wharf,
Droitwich, Worcestershire WR9 7DU
t 01905 771464 **f** 01905 771464
e slater_janet@hotmail.com
Retail/mail order, wide selection. Dyes, fabrics,
threads, silk/linen supplier. Also gallery,
cushions, bags, waistcoats, wallhangings, etc.

Kemtex Colours
Chorley Business & Technology Centre,
Euxton Lane, Chorley, Lancashire PR7 6TE
t 01257 230220 **f** 01257 230225
e www.textiledyes.co.uk
w www.kemtex.co.uk
Suppliers of textile dyes and associated auxiliary
products plus series of introductory dyeing kits.

Mulberry Silks/Mulberry Papers
2 Old Rectory Cottages, Easton Grey,
Malmesbury, Wiltshire SN16 0PE
t 01666 840881 **f** 01666 841028
e patricia.wood@rdplus.net
w www.mulberrysilks-patriciawood.com
Mulberry silks supplies embroidery silk in
beautiful colour sets. SAE for price list please.

Omega Dyes (Bailey Curtis)
10 Corsend Road, Hartpury, Glos GL19 3BP
t 01452 700492 **f** 01452 700492
e bailey@omegadyes.co.uk
w www.omegadyes.co.uk
Omega Dyes offers a good selection of 4 different
dye types, which colour a wide variety of fibres
and fabrics. See also Textile Artists and
Designers; ad p. 39.

Silk Gallery
The Stables, Nannerch, Mold CH7 5RD
t 01352 741893
e bev@silkgallery.org.uk
w www.silkgallery.org.uk
Ready-to-paint silk wall hangings. SAE for details
and prices. See also Textile Artists & Designers.

Tamar Embroideries
Little Honeycombe, Tamar Way, Gunnislake,
Cornwall PL18 9DH
t 01822 833099
e sales@TamarEmbroideries.co.uk
w www.TamarEmbroideries.co.uk
*Mail order supplies of silk painting and textile
art materials.*

Vycombe Arts
14 Orchid Way, Needham Market, Suffolk
IP6 8JQ
t 01449 722220 **f** 01449 722220
e vycombe_Arts@btconnect.com
*Beautiful silks, paints, dyes and fabric
embellishments for transforming your dreams
into creations. Mail order - postage and package
free. See ad on p.34.*

Embroidery

Anna Pearson Needlepoint Design
The Studio, Grymsdyke Farm, Lacey Green,
Bucks HP27 0RB
t 01844 347477 **f** 01844 274249
e anna@needle-point.co.uk
w www.needle-point.co.uk
*Distinctive needlepoint designs and classes in
many parts of the country. Kits by mail order.
Custom design.*

Celtic Threads
Rhoslwyn, Maes Tegid, Bala, Gwynedd
LL23 7BJ
t 01678 520027 **f** 01678 520027
e mail@celticthreads.co.uk
w www.celticthreads.co.uk
*Specialist supplier of materials for lacemaking
and fine traditional embroidery.*

(The) Crewel Work Company Ltd
Pembroke House, 1 Clifford Street, Appleby
in Westmorland, Cumbria CA16 6TS
t 01768 353683 **f** 01768 353683
e info@crewelwork.co.uk
w www.crewelwork.co.uk
*Specially woven Jacobean linen twill. Crewel
work kits. Workshops in design and technique.
Exhibition: 300 years of British crewel work.*

Dinsdale Embroideries
13 Castle Close, Middleton St George,
Darlington, County Durham DL2 1DE
t 01325 332592 **f** 01325 335704
e admin@DinsdaleEmbroideries.co.uk
w www.DinsdaleEmbroideries.co.uk
*Goldwork, pulled work and other kits. Metal
threads, pearl cotton etc. Dayschools held
month-ly on various techniques. Weekly classes.*

Gillsew
Boundary House, Moor Common, Lane End,
Bucks HP14 3HR
e gillsew@ukonline.co.uk
*As well as a good range of products, I sell trial
size packs of many items, at trial size prices.*

Glitterati Crafts
Suite 9 - Unit 1, Flexi Offices, 1000 North
Circular Road, London, NW2 7JP
t 020 8208 2232 **f** 020 8208 1233
e glitterati2001@aol.com
w www.glitterati-crafts.com
*Everything that glitters!! Motifs, bells, mesh, fabric
pieces, braids, threads, accessories. Indian rayon,
Natesh, in 220 shades including 40 variegated.*

Golden Threads
Spotted Cow Cottage, Broad Oak,
Heathfield, East Sussex TN21 8UE
t 01435 862810
e info@goldenthreads.co.uk
w www.goldenthreads.co.uk
*Supplier of metallic embroidery threads, trim-
mings, goldwork kits and sundry embroidery
materials. Talks given on history of gold threads.*

Hanging by a Thread
PO Box 10723, London SE3 0ZL
t 020 8318 1337
e hbat10723@aol.com
w www.hangingbyathread.net
*Counted thread embroidery classes and weekends.
Visiting American teachers twice a year. Will also
consider travelling to teach groups/guilds.*

please let them know you found
their number in
the textile directory 2003

thank you

Isis Designs
(Dept TD) PO Box 268, Bridgwater, Somerset
TA6 6YJ
t 07831 733652
*We supply unusual packs of fabrics, threads,
beads, sequins, etc. in small quantities, at low
prices. Also inspirational packages/kits.*

Ivy House Studio
37 High Street, Kessingland, Suffolk
NR33 7QQ
t 01502 740414
e janet_hawkes@lineone.net
*48-page catalogue, surface design, bonding,
burning. Shrinking, expanding, stitching,
fabrics, threads. Send 4 x 1st class stamps - fast
and friendly service.*

Kates Kloths
58 Regent Street, Blyth, Northumberland
NE24 1LT
e 01670 354342
*Wide range of hand-dyed variegated threads/
fabrics. Experimental fabrics - jute, scrim,
fleece, silk fibres. Send large SAE for
mail-order catalogue.*

Madeira Threads
Thirsk Industrial Park, York Road, Thirsk,
North Yorkshire YO7 3BX
t 01845 524880 f 01845 525046
e info@madeira.co.uk
w www.madeira.co.uk
Manufacturers of embroidery and sewing thread.

Margaret Beal Embroidery
28 Leigh Road, Andover, Hants SP10 2AP
t 01264 365102 f 01264 365102
e margaret.beal@onet.co.uk
*Soldering irons. Acrylic felt. Fabric. 'Burning
Issues' day schools - cutting, bonding and mark-
making. See ad on p. 30.*

(The) Mulberry Dyer
Maes Gwyn Rhewl, Ruthin, Denbighshire
LL15 1UL
t 01824 703616
e fishwife@mulberrydyer.co.uk
w mulberrydyer.co.uk
*Supplier to spinners, dyers, embroiderers and
knitters. Stock includes silks, wools,
embroidery and knitting kits, spindles, carders
and natural dyes.*

Perfect Pearls
20 Admiral Gardens, Cowes, Isle of Wight
PO31 7XE
t 01983 294096 f 01983 294096
e perfectpearls@zoom.co.uk
*Top-quality loose freshwater pearls. Experiment
with a sample pack (24 pearls, various sizes).
£5.00 inc. postage.*

Prospects
Prospect House, Smithy Lane, Preesall,
Poulton-le-Fylde, Lancashire FY6 0NQ
t 01253 811523
*For a free brochure, please send A5 stamped
addressed envelope.*

Silken Strands
20, Y Rhos, Bangor, Gwynedd LL57 2LT
e silkenstrands@yahoo.co.uk
w www.silkenstrands.co.uk
t 01248 362361 f 01248 362361
*Threads by Madeira, DMC, YLI, Oliver Twist,
disappearing fabrics, pens and thread, and all
embroidery requisites.*

TC Threads Limited
Mancor House, Bolsover Street, Hucknall,
Nottinghamshire NG15 7TZ
t 0115 968 0089 f 0115 968 0346
e sales@tcthreads.ltd.uk
w www.tcthreads.ltd.uk
*Suppliers of threads and accessories to the embroi-
dery trade, involving needles, scissors, interlin-
ings, felt, bobbins, adhesives and lubricants.*

(The) Thread Studio
e mail@thethreadstudio.com
w www.thethreadstudio.com
See Websites, p. 110 for full contact details
*Speciality embroidery threads and textile art sup-
plies by mail order. Our shop is in cyberspace.
Also 'Playways on the Net' textile art course.*

Variegations
Rose Cottage, Harper Royd Lane, Norland,
Halifax HX6 3QQ
t 01422 832411
e variegat@globalnet.co.uk
w www.variegations.com
*Bonding, burning, printing, dyeing, painting,
stitching, shrinking, discharging, dissolving -
Variegations can supply the goods. 4 x 1st class
stamps for catalogue. See also Shops (Embroidery).*

Vari-Galore (Lorna Bateman)
5 Bennet Close, Alton, Hants GU34 2EL
t 01420 80595 **f** 01420 80595
e lorna@varigalore.com
w www.varigalore.com
Large range of imported South African hand-dyed threads, silk ribbons, embroidery kits, buttons and books. Lessons, lectures and workshops. See also Textile Artists and Designers; ad p. 34.

Wern Mill Gallery and Textile Craft Workshops
Melin-y-Wern, Denbigh Road, Nannerch, Mold, Flintshire CH7 5RH, Wales
t 01352 741318 **f** 01352 741318
e chrisatwernmill@tiscali.co.uk
w www.wernmillcreative.co.uk
Wern Mill Creative; new 'free' machine embroidery kits. Original designs by textile artist Christine Garwood. All materials, full instructions supplied. See also Textile Artists and Designers.

World Embroidery
2 Woodlands, Kirby Misperton, Malton, North Yorkshire YO17 6XW
t 01653 697254
e worldembroidery@kirbymisperton.freeserve.co.uk
Beads, bells, shells, shisha and hand-dyed fabrics. All sorts of unusual things for stitchers! See also Beads, Beads, Beads; Foreign Textile Studies.

Fabrics

Euro Japan Links Ltd
32 Nant Road, Childs Hill, London NW2 2AT
t 020 8201 9324 **f** 020 8201 9324
e eurojpn@aol.com
Modern and traditional Japanese cottons, sashiko cloth and threads, silk kimono pieces, Japanese embroidery flat silks and metallics

Fabrics for Fun/Beads for Beauty
32 Babbacombe Road, Torquay TQ1 3SN
t 01803 328902 **f** 01803 328902
e charles@wraymccann.freeserve.co.uk
Fabrics in project size pieces - silk, organza, c hif-fon, glitz. Beads, craft wires, bead kits. Embroidery and beading workshop programme. 4 x 27p stamps please. See also Beads, Beads, Beads.

Fantasy Fabrics
Dept TD, Unit 5, Parade Spur North, Pinefield Industrial Estate, Elgin IV30 6AL
t 01343 556000 **f** 01343 556000
e fantasyfabrics@talk21.com
w www.fantasyfabrics.ic24.net
Exotic materials in small pieces, lots of trial packs, chiffon scarves. Free brochure or £3 for catalogue and samples, refundable.

Interlinings Direct
West Holme, London Rd, Rockbeare, Exeter, Devon EX5 2DZ
t 01404 822158
e interlinings@btopenworld.com
Quality European interlinings/stabilisers for today's fabrics. Dressmaking, tailoring, soft furnishing, embroidery; modern and traditional. Friendly needlework clubs held weekly.

Pennine Outdoor Fabrics
Yew Tree Mills, Holmbridge, Holmfirth HD9 2NN
t 01484 689100 **f** 01484 689101
e sales@pennineoutdoor.co.uk
w www.pennineoutdoor.co.uk
Major stockists of fleece, waterproof breathable and tent fabrics, including zips, thread, buckles and webbing. For all your outdoor requirements.

Silk Route
Cross Cottage, Cross Lane, Frimley Green, Surrey GU16 6LN
t 01252 835781
e hilary@thesilkroute.co.uk
w www.thesilkroute.co.uk
Specialist in natural and coloured silk fabrics for embroidery, patchwork, quilting, dolls, miniature furnishings, etc.

Whaleys (Bradford) Ltd
Harris Court, Great Horton, Bradford BD7 4EQ
t 01274 **f** 01274 **f** 01274 521309
e whaleys@btinternet.com
w www.whaleys-bradford.ltd.uk
Specialist suppliers of natural fabrics for printing, dyeing and craft Cottons, wool, silk, etc. 450 qualities in stock.

General Needlecraft

Artika Designs/Linda Jackson
The Old Rectory, Combpyne, Axminster,
Devon EX13 8SY
t 01297 443918 f 01297 445029
e artika@compuserve.com
w www.artika.co.uk
*Booklets of original abstract charted designs,
including Art Deco, Optical Illusions, Animal
Prints and Patchwork Designs. Catalogue on website. See also Mail Order Suppliers (Knitting/
Crochet; Rugmaking); Textile Artists & Designers.*

Focus Needlecraft Wholesale
Hardwicke Ind Est, Hardwicke Stables,
Hadnall, Shrewsbury, Shropshire, SY4 4AS
t 01939 210790 f 01939 210796
*Mail order suppliers of haberdashery, needlecraft
products, knitting wool and knitting accessories
to trade and educational outlets.*

Heart of England Sewing Machines
Beechcroft, Worcester Rd, Inkberrow WR7 4EX
t 01386 793991 f 01386 793911
e pandpmay@aol.com
*Importer/wholesaler to schools, embroiderers,
City & Guilds. Machines, haberdashery, threads,
beads, multicultural embellishments.Free
catalogue. Visitors: appointment only.*

Henley Needlecrafts
31 Deanfield Ave, Henley-on-Thames RG9 1UE
t 01491 410840/410162
*Supplies, cushion-making and framing.
Individual and group classes on demand -
canvaswork, cross stitch, embroidery, etc. B & B
in Henley if required.*

Hopkaji Designs
11 Ashbrow Road, Northampton NN4 8ST
t 01604 459591
*Cross stitch company specialising in Native
American designs. Also have small Celtic and
children's ranges. All designs original.*

Lazy Daisy Designs
Keepers Cottage, Leechpond Hill, Lower
Beeding, Horsham, West Sussex RH13 6NR
t 01403 891516
e lazydaisydesigns@aol.com
w www.lazydaisy.freeserve.co.uk
*Cross stitch & crafts - to make or give complete! Baby
blankets, greetings cards and anything to order!*

Siesta
Unit D, Longmeadow Works, Ringwood Rd,
Three Legged Cross, Wimborne, Dorset
BH21 6RD
t 01202 813363
e sales@siestaframes.com
w www.siestaframes.com
*Working frames, stands, magnifiers, lights and
accessories. For cross stitch, needlecraft, silk
painting and quilting.*

Sue B Sew
The Old School Room, Boyles School, High
St, Yetminster, Sherborne, Dorset DT9 6LF
t 01935 873673
e suebsew@totalise.co.uk
*Discount fabric/thread packs for students. Up to
20% off certain lines.*

Village Needlecraft
3 Beaumont Road, Horwich, Bolton, Lancs
BL6 7BG
t 01204 690906
e anneperry@villageneedlecraft.freeserve.co.uk
w www.villageneedlecraft.com
*Canal maps and scenes designed in CCS/LS
linking the history and popularity of waterways.
Also greetings cards, Halls, Leverhulmes
Rivington.*

Willow Fabrics
95, Town Lane, Mobberley, Knutsford,
Cheshire WA16 7HH
t 01565 872225 f 01565 872239
e care@willowfabrics.com
w www.willowfabrics.com
*Huge selection of needlework supplies: Zweigart
fabrics, Anchor yarns, charts, kits, accessories for
cross stitch, tapestry, crochet, etc. Secure website.*

Winifred Cottage

17 Elms Road, Fleet, Hampshire GU51 3EG
t 01252 617667
e winifcott@aol.com
*Mail order supplies for textile artists world-wide
including machine/hand threads, chiffon scarves,
beads, dyes, etc. Email for price list.*

Kit Specialists

Abacus Designs
11 Lime Grove Walk, Matlock, Derbyshire
DE4 3FD
t 01629 760900 **f** 01629 56576
e sales@abacusdesigns.com
w www.abacusdesigns.com
*Cross stitch kits - historic and well-known
buildings, town and coastal scenes, canals and
inland waterways. Tartans. 'Coronation Street'.
'Emmerdale'.*

Animal Fayre ⓣ
Ashwood Cottage, 11 High Cottages,
Walkerburn, Peebleshire EH43 6AZ
t 01896 870754
e animalfayre@tinyworld.co.uk
w www.tapestrykit.com
*A unique collection of cross-stitch tapestry kits.
Tapestries inspired by ancient and mediaeval art
and sewn using rich jewel colours.*

Charlotte's Web Needlework
PO Box 771, Harrow, Middlesex HA2 7WE
t 020 8869 9400 **f** 020 8869 9410
e info@charlotteswebneedlework.com
w www.charlotteswebneedlework.com
*Sophisticated cross stitch kits and charts for
beginners to serious stitchers. These include
heart, floral and Mackintosh-inspired designs.*

(The) Craft Kit Company
t 01306 742310 **f** 01306 742193
e yvonne@thecraftkitcompany.co.uk
w www.thecraftkitcompany.co.uk
*We offer inspiring craft kits and bead storage
systems including a useful range of small, hinged
boxes and carry cases.*

Jill Milne, Jazz Design ⓣ
12 Newcastle Road, Congleton, Cheshire
CW12 4HJ
t 01260 278526 **f** 01260 278526
e jill@jazz-design.com
w www.jazz-design.com
*Unusual needlepoint tapestry and embroidery
kits, inspired by landscapes, pottery and
paintings. Worked in wools and hand-dyed
variegated threads.*

Masterplan (Cross Stitch Kits UK)
Mill Cottage, Mill Lane, Bolton-le-Sands,
Carnforth, Lancashire LA5 8ET
t 01524 734475 **f** 01524 734475
e masterplan@cross-stitch-kits.co.uk
w www.cross-stitch-kits.co.uk
*Original cross-stitch designs to suit all tastes
and abilities. Mail order, wholesale, etc.*

Sarah May Designs Ltd ⓣ
5 Pettiphers Farm, Pebworth, Stratford-
upon-Avon, Warwickshire CV37 8AW
t 01789 720617 **f** 01789 720617
e sales@needlecraft.org
w www.needlecraft.org
*Embroidery designers of cross stitch, blackwork,
Hardanger, surface, crewel and decorative
embroidery. Also extensive range of pewter
needlework giftware.*

Tom Pudding Designs
PO Box 21657, London SW16 1WH
t 020 8769 2558 **f** 020 8769 9713
e jan@tompudding.co.uk
w www.tompudding.co.uk
*Jan Eaton's original chart packs for cross stitch,
blackwork and needlepoint. Visit our website for
online catalogue and free charts.*

Travellers Tales
6 Cheyne Close, Gerrards Cross,
Buckinghamshire SL9 7LG
t 01753 886371 **f** 01753 886371
e travellerstales@europe.com
*An exciting range of cross-stitch kits with
embellishments, based on ethnic and historical
embroideries from all over the world.*

Knitting/Crochet

Andru Knitwear
Poultry Farm, Milton, Brampton, Cumbria
CA8 1HS
t 01697 747571 **f** 01697 747571
e andruchapman@yahoo.co.uk
w www.andruchapman.com
*Originally designed patterns with yarn for hand
and machine knitters. Finest silks to chunky
Egyptian cotton for all textile uses.*

Bringing you the Best in Quality Quilt Festivals for 14 Years

Enter our World of Quilts and the Textile Arts

- Home Page
- About Us
- Quilt Festivals
- Sponsors
- Online Gallery
- Merchants Mall
- Online Newsletter
- Antiques Shows & Other Events
- Vendor Information
- Contact Us

Quilt Show Calendar

Pacific International Quilt Festival
Santa Clara (Bay Area), CA

Williamsburg Festival Week
Mid-Atlantic Quilt Festival
Williamsburg, VA

The Quilt & Sewing Fest at Myrtle Beach
Myrtle Beach, SC

World Quilt & Textile
On Tour: 2003

Pennsylvania National Quilt Extravaganza
Fort Washington (Phila. Area), PA

Founding Sponsors

Nothing Sews Like A Bernina. Nothing.
BERNINA

QUILTER'S NEWSLETTER MAGAZINE

Fairfield

Major Sponsors

Husqvarna VIKING

Pacesetter BY brother elna

baby lock

COATS Coats & Clark

P&B TEXTILES   C&T PUBLISHING INC.

Click here to order a brochure.

Click here to be added to our Email list.

Search our Website

| World Quilt | GO |

To order a printed brochure send $2 (specify event) to:

MANCUSO Show Management

Dept. TD
PO Box 667
New Hope, PA 18938

www.quiltfest.com

Artika Designs/Linda Jackson

The Old Rectory, Combpyne, Axminster,
Devon EX13 8SY
t 01297 443918 **f** 01297 445029
e artika@compuserve.com
w www.artika.co.uk
*Original stitchpatterns for machine knitters and
handknitters including Art Deco, Optical
Illusions, Japanese Designs, Animal Prints, etc.
Catalogue on our website. See also Mail Order
Suppliers (General Needlecraft; Rugmaking);
Textile Artists and Designers.*

Design by Heathmor

Denmor, Herschell Square, Walmer, Deal,
Kent CT14 7SH
t 01304 366770 **f** 01304 366770
*Individually designed knitwear for ladies, gents,
children in Aran, d/k, mohair. Also decorated sweat-
shirts and T-shirts using appliqué and diamanté.*

Edward Hill & Co Ltd

Hollings Mill, Lower Grattan Rd, Bradford
BD1 2JA
t 01274 727283
Suppliers to the craft and handknitting industry.

Forge Craft Creations

The Old Smithy, Pirton, Nr Worcester WR8 9EJ
t 01905 820482
e ForgeCrafts@TheOldSmithy.co.uk
w www.forgecrafts.com
*Swiss darned embroidery kits, knitting patterns
(made to measure) and books.*

Garthenor Organic Pure Wool

Garthenor, Llanio Rd, Tregaron, Dyfed
SY25 6UR
t 01570 493347 **f** 01570 493347
e garthenor@organicpurewool.co.uk
w www.organicpurewool.co.uk
*A wide range of knitting yarns in natural white
and undyed colours, from pure bred certified
organically reared British sheep. See also Mail
Order Suppliers (Weaving/Spinning/
Feltmaking).*

(The) House of Hemp (Jane Blonder)

Beeston Farm, Marhamchurch, Bude,
Cornwall EX23 0ET
t 01288 381638
e jane@thehouseofhemp.co.uk
w www.thehouseofhemp.co.uk
*Organic hemp yarn in beautiful colours. A breath-
able, durable and wearable fibre for hand crafted
garments. See also Textile Artists & Designers;
Mail Order (Weaving/Spinning/Felt); ad on p. 47.*

Hush Knit Yarns

57 Burnside Drive, Bramcote Hills, Beeston,
Notts NG9 3EF
t 0115 922 3654 **f** 0115 922 3654
*Mail order and trade supplier of knitting yarns
for home knitting machines. Organisers of two
shows for machine knitters.*

Jamieson & Smith (Shetland Wool Brokers) Ltd

90 North Rd, Lerwick, Shetland ZE1 0PQ
t 01595 693579 **f** 01595 695009
e shetland.wool.brokers@zetnet.co.uk
w www.shetland-wool-brokers.zetnet.co.uk
*100% wool knitting yarns from chunky to
cobweb. Shade cards £3.00. Also knitting
patterns, raw fleece and combed tops.*

JTD Ltd

34 Cranmore Road, Wolverhampton,
West Midlands WV3 9NL
t 01902 653667 **f** 01902 653668
e info@knitware.co.uk *or* info@bondknitting.com
w www.knitware.co.uk *or* www.bondknitting.com
*UK agent for knitware software and Bond
knitting machine supplies.*

KCG Trading Limited

PO Box 145, Leeds LS8 2WS
t 0113 266 4651
e kcgtl2000@hotmail.com
w www.kcgtrading.com
*Knitting and crochet supplies by mail order. UK
distributor of Margaret Stove Artisan Lace
Weight Merino yarn.*

Knitwell By Post

116 Sunbridge Road, Bradford BD1 2NF
t 01274 722290
*Mail order catalogue offering large selection of
hand knitting yarns, knitting books and leaflets
plus needlecraft kits.*

Manjolyn's Designs
c/o 2 Park View, Hill House, Bushley,
Tewkesbury GL20 6AF
t 07778 286093
e amandaeaglestone@btinternet.com
*From our flock of Suffolk cross ewes. This variety
gives a beautiful soft, silver fleck feel throughout
with an Aran texture. See ad on p. 46.*

Rowan and Jaeger Handknits
Green Lane Mill, Holmfirth, W Yorks HD9 2DX
t 01484 681881 **f** 01484 687920
e mail@knitrowan.com
w www.knitrowan.com
*The best in handknitting design with a range of
knitting magazines, beautiful yarns and knitting
courses nationwide. See also Adult and Further
Education; Publications; Websites.*

Shades of Cashmere
Grove Farm, Wolvey, Hinckley LE10 3LL
t 01455 220767
*Supplier of pure cashmere and cashmere blend
yarns and patterns suitable for the machine or
hand knitter by mail order.*

Uppingham Yarns
North Street East, Uppingham, Rutland
LE15 9QL
t 01572 823747
e uppyarn@wools.co.uk
w www.wools.co.uk
*From acrylic to cashmere, all types of yarns in
various colours and thicknesses for knitters,
weavers, crochet. Accessories too.*

Worth Knitting
Ground Floor 115, Barkby Road, Leicester
LE4 9LG
t 0116 274 0661 **f** 0116 246 0716
e worthknitting@ncyarns.co.uk
w www.ncyarnsltd.sagenet.co.uk
*Our aim is to sell all types of yarn at the
cheapest price to the domestic knitting market.*

Yeoman Yarns Ltd
36 Churchill Way, Fleckney, Leicester LE8 8UD
t 0116 240 4464 **f** 0116 240 2522
e sales@yeomanyarns.co.uk
w www.yeoman-yarns.co.uk
*Yarns for machine/hand knitters/homecrafts.
Cottons, acrylics, fancies, metallics, wools. Our
full set of shade cards £4.95 UK postage free.*

Lace/Tatting

Hilkar Lace Supplies
359 Pentregethin Road, Manselton, Swansea
SA5 8AJ
t 07929 310140
e hilkar@ntlworld.com
*Bobbin lace classes every Monday & Tuesday.
Also full lace supplies: cottons, glass
paperweights, beads, bobbins, pins, etc.!!!*

Jo Firth Lacemaking and Needlecraft Supplies
58 Kent Crescent, Lowtown, Pudsey,
West Yorkshire LS28 9EB
t 0113 257 4881 **f** 0113 257 4881
e jo.firth@cwctv.net
*Lacemaking (bobbin and needle), tatting,
miniature and specialist threads, delica and Mill
Hill beads, fabrics, kits and unusual items.*

Patchwork and Quilting

Custom Quilting Ltd
Beal na Tra, Derrymihan West,
Castletownbere, Co Cork, Ireland
t +353 27 70414 **f** +353 27 70938
e patches@iol.ie
w www.customquilt.com
*Professional quilting service, commission quilts,
UK and European distributor for Gammill
Quilting Machines, longarm quilting workshops,
UK distributor for Aurifil Threads.*

Quilters Cupboard
78 Marldon Road, Paignton, Devon TQ3 3NW
t 01803 528382
e enquiries@quilterscupboard.co.uk
*We specialise in folk art fabrics and folk art kits.
Also hand-dyed fabrics, floral appliqué designs.*

Ribbons

Crafty Ribbons
3 Beechwood, Clump Farm, Tin Pot Lane,
Blandford, Dorset DT11 7TS
t 01258 455889
e info@craftyribbons.com
w www.craftyribbons.com
*Satins, wire edged, ombre, chiffon, gold, silver,
plain, floral, patterned, narrow, wide, whatever
your ribbon needs contact Crafty Ribbons!*

Nostalgia
147a Nottingham Road, Eastwood,
Nottingham
t 01773 712240 f 01773 712240
e robert@nostalgiaribbon.freeserve.co.uk
*Hand-dyed ribbon, silk, wire edge, mukuba
ribbons, lace, trims, beads, purse frames, silk
prints, velvet leaves, charms, beaded flowers.*

Ribbon Designs
PO Box 382, Edgware, Middlesex HA8 7XQ
t 020 8958 4966 f 020 8958 4966
e info@silkribbon.co.uk
*Pure silk, satin and organdy ribbons, sold by
the metre, by the reel or in inspiring mixed
assortments.*

Rugmaking

Artika Designs/Linda Jackson
The Old Rectory, Combpyne, Axminster,
Devon EX13 8SY
t 01297 443918 f 01297 445029
e artika@compuserve.com
w www.artika.co.uk
*Original abstract charted designs suitable for
rugmakers, including Art Deco, Optical
Illusions, Animal Prints and Patchwork Designs.
Catalogue at www.Artika.co.uk See also Mail
Order Suppliers (Knitting/Crochet; General
Needlecraft); Textile Artists and Designers; .*

Diane Dorward
27 Hawkwood Close, Malvern,
Worcestershire WR14 1QU
t 01684 564056
e diane.dorward@virgin.net
*Workshops and supplies for rag rug making,
stencilling and other crafts. Send SAE for our
illustrated mail order catalogue.*

Sewing Machine Sales

Sewing Machines Direct
Wentworth, Bannell Lane, Penymynydd,
Chester CH4 0EP
t 08000 925215
e enquiries@sewingmachines.direct.co.uk
w www.sewingmachinesdirect.co.uk
*The original sewing machine mail order
specialist. Supplier of quality sewing machines,
overlockers, cabinets and ironing presses.*

Smocking

House of Smocking
1 Ryeworth Road, Charlton Kings,
Cheltenham, Gloucestershire GL52 6LG
t 01242 245204
e chris@smocking.co.uk
w www.smocking co.uk
*Smocking classes, mail order smocking supplies
of pleaters, transfer dots, patterns, books,
magazines, fine piping, lace. Callers welcome by
appointment.*

Soft Furnishing

Interiors at Home
6 Central Avenue, Welling, Kent DA16 3BB
t 020 8317 0341 f 020 8317 0762
e enq@interiorsathome.co.uk
w www.interiorsathome.co.uk
*For poles, fabrics, linings, bedspreads, throws,
cushions, readymades, nets, blinds, trimmings
and wallpaper. Check out our secure mail order
website.*

Stands/Furniture/Lights

The Craft Chest
Hotley Bottom Lane, Prestwood, Bucks
HP16 9PL
t 01494 866768
e thecraftchest@aol.com
*Elegant English-built furniture designed to take
all your craft needs but also to grace any room in
your home.*

The Daylight Company Ltd

89-91 Scrubs Lane, London NW10 6QU
t 020 8964 1200 **f** 020 8964 1300
e daylight@btinternet.com
w www.daylightcompany.com
Textile enthusiasts will love our Daylight simulation lamps and magnifiers. They provide excellent colour matching, increased clarity and reduced eye strain.

Facades

PO Box 162, Brayford, Barnstaple, Devon
EX32 7YH
t 01598 710900 **f** 01598 710813
e enquiries@facades-devon.co.uk
w www.facades-devon.co.uk
We make and design a range of handcrafted sewing workstations, cutting tables, etc. Custom service also available - studios and workrooms.

Threads

Beginnings

Powells, Staplegrove Road, Taunton,
Somerset TA2 6AL
t 01823 275942
Suppliers of hand-dyed threads and fabric, fancy fabrics, etc. Plus various kits for books and cushions by mail order.

Oliver Twists

22 Phoenix Road, Crowther, Washington,
Tyne and Wear NE38 0AD
t 0191 416 6016 **f** 0191 415 3405
e jean@olivertwists.freeserve.co.uk
Producers of variegated hand-dyed threads, fabrics and fibres.

Riitta Sinkkonen Davies ⓣ

Mathom House, Moorland Road, Freystop,
Haverfordwest, Pembrokeshire SA62 4LE
t 01437 890712 **f** 01437 890712
e riitta@rasdavies.co.uk
w www.rasdavies.co.uk
Finnish linen tow yarns in beautiful colours. Also flax for handspinning and feltmaking. Please send £2.50 for shade cards.

From our flock of Suffolk Cross Ewes, this variety gives a beautiful soft, silver fleck feel throughout with an Aran texture

Manjolyn's Designs

- Suppliers of high quality pure wool.
- In stock a Range of tested patterns for working our own wool.
- Wool is supplied in 100gm Hanks.
- Colour card available.
- Wool in two colours; Dark and Light.

Contact us for more information:
Manjolyn's Designs
2 Park View, Hill House, Bushley
Tewkesbury, Glos GL20 6AF
Tel: Jo 07778 286093 Mandy 01452 840132

Weaving/Spinning/Feltmaking

Crafty Notions ⓣ

104 Middleton Road, Newark, Notts
NG24 2DN
t 01636 659890
e enquiries@craftynotions.com
w www.craftynotions.com
Mail order - hard-to-find supplies and fibres for felting and embroidery.

Garthenor Organic Pure Wool

Garthenor, Llanio Road, Tregaron, Dyfed
SY25 6UR
t 01570 493347 **f** 01570 493347
e garthenor@organicpurewool.co.uk
w www.organicpurewool.co.uk
A wide range of organic fleece, raw and carded, in natural undyed colours, from pure-bred certified British sheep. See also Mail Order Suppliers (Knitting/Crochet).

Hilltop **t**

Windmill Cross, Canterbury Road, Lyminge,
Folkestone, Kent CT18 8HD
t 01303 862617
e info@handspin.co.uk
w www.handspin.co.uk
Specialists in spinning, weaving and related
textile craft supplies and tuition. Free mail order
brochure. See also Private Colleges, Publications,
Specialist Breaks, Textile Tours and Websites; ad
below left.

(The) House of Hemp (Jane Blonder) **t**

Beeston Farm, Marhamchurch, Bude,
Cornwall EX23 0ET
t 01288 381638
e jane@thehouseofhemp.co.uk
w www.thehouseofhemp.co.uk
Organic hemp yarn in natural and a range of
beautiful colours for weavers. See also Mail
Order Suppliers (Knitting/Crochet); Textile
Artists and Designers; ad below right.

Natural Yarns **t**

19 Minching Close, York, North Yorkshire
YO30 5GL
t 01347 868231
e info@naturalyarns.co.uk
We sell pure wool and fleeces, raw and carded
from rare breeds of sheep.

Sarah Stacey Hedgehog Equipment **t**

Daren Uchaf, Cwmyoy, Abergavenny,
Monmouthshire NP7 7NR
t 01873 890712 **f** 01873 890712
e sarah@hedgehogequipment.co.uk
w www.hedgehogequipment.co.uk
Manufacturers of hedgehog carding, spinning,
weaving and felting equipment. UK agent for
Majacraft spinning wheels and accessories
and windwool fibres. **t**

The Handweavers Studio

29 Haroldstone Road, London E17 7AN
t 020 8521 2281
e handweaversstudio@msn.com
w www.handweaversstudio.co.uk
Spinning/weaving/felting supplies and tuition.
Fibres, fleeces, yarns, equipment, books and dyes.
Mail order and personal callers. Est. 1973.

Museums

(The) Allhallows Museum
High Street, Honiton, Devon EX14 1PG
e 01404 44966 f 01404 46591
e info@allhallowsmuseum.co.uk
w www.allhallowsmuseum.co.uk
A world-class collection of lace is kept and displayed along with local antiquities in a former chapel of mediaeval origin.

(The) American Museum in Britain
Claverton Manor, Bath BA2 7BD
t 01225 460503 f 01225 469160
e amibbath@aol.com
w www.americanmuseum.org
Most important collection of American textiles outside USA: 200 quilts; woven coverlets; samplers; hooked rugs; Navajo weaving (84 on view).

Antonio Ratti Textile Center
The Metropolitan Museum of Art,
1000 Fifth Avenue at 82nd Street, New York NY 10028-0198, USA
t 1 212 650 2310 f 1 212 650 2676
e Ratti.Center@metmuseum.org
w www.metmuseum.org
The Ratti Textile Center houses the Metropolitan Museum of Art's textile collections. Image database, library and viewing sessions by appointment.

Bankfield Museum (t)
Akroyd Park, Boothtown Road, Halifax, West Yorkshire HX3 6HG
t 01422 352334/354823 f 01422 349020
e bankfield_museum@calderdale.gov.uk
w www.calderdale.gov.uk/imadethat/
An internationally important collection of textiles, costume and crafts (historic, multicultural and contemporary) plus temporary exhibitions and active education programme.

(The) Bear Museum
38 Dragon Street, Petersfield GU31 4JJ
t 01730 265108
e judy@bearmuseum.co.uk
w www.bearmuseum.co.uk
The first museum in the world for teddy bears. Examples of most types on show. Also Steiff replicas and others for sale.

(The) Bowes Museum (t)
Barnard Castle, Co Durham DL12 8NP
t 01833 690606 f 01833 637163
e info@bowesmuseum.org.uk
w www.bowesmuseum.org.uk
Magnificent French chateau having European fine and decorative art, tapestries, embroideries, quilts, lace, carpets, costume. Programme of special exhibitions with workshops.

Braintree District Museum & Study (t) Centre Trust
Manor Street, Braintree, Essex
t 01376 325266 f 01376 344345
e jean@bdcmuseum.demon.co.uk
Permanent displays on local silk and man-made textile industries (Warners/Courtaulds). Changing exhibition programme throughout the year.

Colour Museum, Society of Dyers and (t) Colourists
Perkin House, PO Box 244, Providence Street, Bradford, West Yorkshire BD1 2PW
t 01274 390955 f 01274 392888
e museum@sdc.org.uk
w www.sdc.org.uk
Colour and textiles gallery. Special textile-based exhibitions, some accompanied by workshops.

Forge Mill Needle Museum (t)
Needle Mill Lane, Riverside, Redditch, Worcestershire B98 8HY
t 01527 62509 f 01527 66721
e museum@redditchbc.gov.uk
w www.redditchbc.gov.uk
Exhibitions of contemporary textiles. Displays about how needles are made. Supplier of specialist needles - shop and mail order. Textile workshop programme. See also Art Galleries and Exhibitions; Shops (General Needlecraft).

Gallery of Costume (t)
Platt Hall, Rusholme, Manchester M14 5LL
t 0161 224 5217 f 0161 256 3278
w www.manchestergalleries.org
From 17th-century embroideries to 21st-century designer costume, including embroideries from India and Pakistan.

Llandudno Museum
17-19 Gloddaeth Street, Llandudno, Conwy
LL30 2DD
t 01492 876517 f 01492 876517
e llandudno.museum@lineone.net
w www.llandudno-tourism.co.uk/museum
*Chardon colection of sculptures, paintings, objets
d'art, ancient and Roman archaeology, town
resort history, Welsh kitchen, war memorabilia,
temporary exhibitions.*

Macclesfield Silk Museums
Park Lane, Macclesfield, Cheshire SK11 6TJ
t 01625 612045 f 01625 612048
e postmaster@silk-macc.u-net.com
w www.silk-macclesfield.org
*History of silk, guided tours with demonstrations
of jacquard handloom weaving, study facilities,
silk shop.*

Manor House Museum 🅣
Honey Hill, Bury St Edmunds, Suffolk
IP33 1HF
t 01284 757072/6 f 01284 747231
e manor.house@burybo.stedsbc.gov.uk
w www.stedmundsbury.gov.uk
*Textile exhibitions covering the Tudor period to
1950s. Regular study sessions, creative beading,
silk embroidery and other workshops and
lectures.*

**Museum of Costume and Fashion
Research Centre**
Assembly Rooms, Bennett Street, Bath BA1
2KH
t 01225 477752 f 01225 444793
e costume_enquiries@bathnes.gov.uk
w www.museumofcostume.co.uk
*The Museum of Costume is one of the finest
collections of fashionable garments in the world.
'Modern Time? People and Dress in 1920s' from
Dec 2002 to Nov 2003.*

National Museums of Scotland
Chambers Street, Edinburgh EH1 1JF
t 0131 225 7534 (voice) 0131 247 4027 (minicom)
f 0131 220 4819
e info@nms.ac.uk
w www.nms.ac.uk
*3 museums in Edinburgh, 1 in New Abbey, 1 in
East Lothian, 1 in East Kilbride.*

Pickford's House Museum
41 Friar Gate, Derby DE1 1DA
t 01332 255363 f 01332 255277
e pickford.house@derby.gov.uk
w www.derby.gov.uk/museums
*Georgian house museum with displays of
historic costume and lively temporary
exhibition programmes which include
contemporary textiles.*

Ryedale Folk Museum 🅣
Hutton le Hole, York YO62 6UA
*Rag rugs on show and occasional rugmaking
demonstrations.*

Shambellie House Museum of Costume
New Abbey, Dumfries, Scotland
t 01387 850375 f 01387 850461
w www.nms.ac.uk
*Victorian country house set in mature
woodlands. Period costumes on open display
with furniture, ceramics and decorative art.*

**Sir Richard Arkwright's Masson Mills
Working Textile Museum**
Derby Road, Matlock Bath, Derbyshire
DE4 3PY
t 01629 581001 f 01629 581001
w www.massonmills.co.uk
*The museum contains a unique and comprehen-
sive collection of authentic working machinery,
illustrating textile designing, spinning and
weaving.*

Temple Newsam House
Leed LS15 0AE
t 0113 264 7321 f 0113 260 2285
e tnewsamho.leeds@virgin.net
w www.leeds.gov.uk/tourinfo/attract
*Historic textile collection. View by appointment
only. (House closed until late 2003.) Catalogue
(400 colour illustrations) available now by post.*

(The) Textile Museum
2320 S Street, NW, Washington, DC 20008-
4088, USA
t +1 202 667 0441 f +1 202 483 0994
e info@textilemuseum.org
w www.textilemuseum.org
*Devoted to the handmade textile arts. Changing
exhibitions cover traditional techniques and
modern masters. Explore the textile learning
centre. Free.*

Ulster Museum, Department of Applied Art

Botanic Gardens, Belfast BT9 5AB
t 028 9038 3072 f 028 9030 3003
e elizabeth.mccrum.um@nics.gov.uk
w www.ulstermuseum.org.uk
The museum holds a large costume and smaller flat textiles collection dating from the 18th century to the present.

Victoria and Albert Museum ⓣ

Cromwell Road, London SW7 2RL
e 020 7942 2197 f 020 7942 2193
w www.vam.ac.uk
Design for Knitting Study Day, 2 November 2002. Art of the Stitch Study Days, 21, 22 March 2003, £35 per day, concessions available.

William Morris Gallery

Lloyd Park, Forest Road, London E17 4PP
t 020 8527 3782 f 020 8527 7070
w www.lbwf.gov.uk/wmg
Permanent displays of work by William Morris, the great Victorian designer-craftsman and by designers of the Arts and Crafts Movement.

Indigo Vessels III & V, Sue Hiley Harris, see Textile Artists and Designers, p. 99.

Worthing Museum & Art Gallery

Chapel Road, Worthing, Sussex BN11 1HP
t 01903 239999 ext. 1139 f 01903 236277
e museum@worthing.gov.uk
Big costume/textile collection, two costume galleries, textile (historic and contemporary) exhibitions and related events; directory of Sussex-based artist makers.

Museums by area

East Anglia

Braintree District Museum & Study Centre Trust
Manor House Museum

Midlands

Forge Mill Needle Museum
Pickford's House Museum
Sir Richard Arkwright's Masson Mills Working Textile Museum

North Central

Temple Newsam House

North East

(The) Bowes Museum
Colour Museum, Society of Dyers and Colourists
Ryedale Folk Museum

North West

Bankfield Museum
Gallery of Costume
Macclesfield Silk Museums

Northern Ireland

Ulster Museum, Department of Applied Art

Scotland

National Museums of Scotland
Shambellie House Museum of Costume

South East

The Bear Museum
Victoria and Albert Museum
William Morris Gallery
Worthing Museum & Art Gallery

South West

The Allhallows Museum
The American Museum in Britain
Museum of Costume and Fashion Research Centre

Wales

Llandudno Museum

USA

Antonio Ratti Textile Center
The Textile Museum

Organisations

Association of Guilds of Weavers, Spinners & Dyers
3 Gatchell Meadow, Trull, Taunton, Somerset TA3 7HY
t 01823 325345
e paddy@bakker.swinternet.co.uk
w WSD.org.uk
Preservation and improvement in handweaving, spinning and dyeing and promotion of public awareness and education.

(The) Batik Guild
16 St Paul's Place, London N1 2QE
t 020 7226 3744 f 020 7226 3744
w www.batikguild.org.uk
Promotes and improves education in the field of batik. Provides members with workshops, meetings and exhibitions.

(The) Beadworkers Guild
PO Box 24922, London, SE23 3WS
t 0870 200 1250
w www.beadworkersguild.org
Promotes the art of beadwork. Tutors' directory, membership directory, educational programme. Organisers of The Great British Bead Show (May 2003). See ad on p. 53.

(The) Braid Society
2 Normanton, Buckland Road, Reigate RH2 9RQ
t 01737 242623
e info@braidsociety.org
w www.braidsociety.org
The Society seeks to generate interest and skills in all aspects of braidmaking including kumihimo, cordmaking, tablet and inkle weaving.

Coats Crafts UK
PO Box 22, Lingfield House, Lingfield Point, McMullen Road, Darlington DL1 1YQ
t 01325 394237 (consumer helpline)
f 01325 394200
e consumer.ccuk@coats.com
w www.coatscrafts.co.uk
Coats Crafts UK is the UK's leading supplier of needlecraft products in the UK. Handicrafts, sewing, haberdashery and handknitting.

Computer Textile Design Group
Galleybirds, Fielden Road, Crowborough, East Sussex TN6 1TP
t 01892 669030 f 01892 611896
e memsec_ctdg@hotmail.com
w www.ctdg.nildram.co.uk
Membership of the Computer Textile Design Group offers information and inspiration to creative textile-minded computer users. See ad on p. 55.

Crafts Council
Reference, 44a Pentonville Road, Islington, London N1 9BY
t 020 7806 2501 f 020 7837 6891
w www.craftscouncil.org.uk
The Crafts Council is the national centre and leading authority of contemporary craft in Great Britain and is based in London.

Embroiderers' Guild
Apartment 41, Hampton Court Palace, Hampton Court, Surrey KT8 9AU
t 020 8943 1229 f 020 8977 9882
e administrator@embroiderersguild.com
w www.embroiderersguild.com
Workshops, exhibitions, events and tours for Guild members and non-members. Specialist bookshop, library and three magazines. Unique museum collection.

Essex Handicrafts Association
c/o Badley Hall, Great Bromley, Colchester, Essex CO7 7UU
e 01206 231262 f 01206 231536
e leonie@essexhandicrafts.org
w www.essexhandicrafts.org
Promotes education in art and crafts in Essex and adjoining counties, particularly in organising classes, day schools, demonstrations and exhibitions.

European Textile Network
PO Box 5944, D-30059 Hannover, Germany
t +49 511 817006 f +49 511 813108
e etn@ETN-net.org
w www.ETN-net.org
550 members in 55 countries, institutions/ individuals from the fields of textile production (arts/crafts/industry), heritage (museums) and education (academies/universities).

Guild of Machine Knitters
c/o Alison Lee (Chairman), 14 Church View
Crescent, Fiskerton, Lincoln LN3 4HL
t 01522 752824
e alison@knitting.freeserve.co.uk
w www.guild-mach-knit.org.uk
*Support, encouragement, education and
comradeship for everyone to enjoy the wonderful
craft of machiine knitting. Come and join us!*

Guild of Needle Laces
36 Cleeve, Tamworth, Staffs B77 2QD
e gnlaces@netscapeonline.co.uk
w http://members.netscapeonline.co.uk/gnlaces
*Promoting the modern uses of the craft of
needle lace.*

(The) Guild of Silk Painters
69 Priory Road, Hastings, East Sussex
TN34 3JJ
f 01424 444464
e editor@silkpainters.guild.co.uk
w www.silkpainters.guild.co.uk
*UK and international membership of around 650
from 30 countries. Quarterly journal in colour
and extensive website with online gallery.
See ad on p. 30.*

International Feltmakers Association
w www.feltmakers.com
*The IFA promotes the art and craft of feltmaking
by organising events, exhibitions and actions for
further interest in feltmaking.*

International Quilts Association
7600 Woodway, Suite 550, Houston TX 77063
USA
t +1 713 781 6882 f +1 713 781 8182
e iqa@quilts.com
w www.quilts.org
*A worldwide organisation of quilt makers, lovers
and collectors.*

(The) Knitting & Crochet Guild
Anne Budworth (Membership Secretary), 108
Park Lane, Kidderminster, Worcs DY11 6TB
t 01562 754367
e budwortha@blueyonder.co.uk
w www.knitting-and-crochet-guild.org.uk
*Quarterly newsletter, Study Day programme,
regional branches, library, helpline, pattern
search service, Young Yarn User newsletter,
educational resource materials.*

(The) Lace Guild
The Hollies, 53 Audnam, Stourbridge,
West Midlands DY8 4AE
t 01384 390739 f 01384 444415
e hollies@.laceguild.org
w www.laceguild.org
*Quarterly magazine; reference and lending
library; extensive study collection of lace,
patterns, tools, etc.; support for contemporary
and traditional lacemaking.*

(The) Lacemakers Circle
44 Ferrers Avenue, Tutbury, Burton-on-Trent
DE13 9JR
t 01283 812477 f 01283 812477
e info@lacemakers-circle.org.uk
w www.lacemakers-circle.org.uk
*A focus for lacemakers, beginners to advanced,
the quarterly magazine has patterns, features,
news, forthcoming events, helpline – library
available.*

Medieval Dress and Textile Society (MEDATS)
c/o Karen Watts, Royal Armouries,
Armouries Drive, Leeds LS10 1LT
w www.medats.cwc.net
*Medats offers a stimulating programme of
meetings for an interested and diverse
membership. A well-informed newsletter is
produced regularly.*

(The) National Needlework Archive
Boldre House, 5 Boldrewood Road,
Southampton, Hampshire SO16 7BW
t 023 8079 1066 f 023 8077 0740
e nna@boldre.freeserve.co.uk
*The NNR archives all needlework throughout
the UK. Also responsible for the national
record of millennium needlework (Stitch 2000
research project).*

OIDFA International Bobbin and Needle Lace Organisation
Nonsuch Too, 27 Ollands Road, Reepham,
Norfolk NR10 4EL
w http://mapage.noos.fr/oidfa
*Hosts a Lace Congress every other year. 2004
Czech Republic. 2006 Greece. Has a quarterly
magazine.*

(The) Quilter's Guild of the British Isles

Room 190, Dean Clough, Halifax HA3 5AX
t 01422 347669 f 01422 345017
e jane@qghalifax.org.uk
w www.quiltersguild.org.uk
Membership organisation welcoming anyone interested in the making, collecting and study of quilts and patchworks, old and new. £26 annually.

Society of Designer Craftsmen

24 Rivington Street, London EC2A 3DU
t 020 7739 2663 f 020 7739 2663
e secretary@societydesigncraft.org.uk
Members design and make original things, including textiles. The Society organises the 'Designer Crafts', annual exhibition at The Mall Galleries, London.

Suffolk Crafts Society

Bridge Green Farm, Gissing Road, Burston IP22 5UD
t 01379 740711 f 01379 740711
e organiser@suffolkcraftsociety.org
w www.suffolkcraftsociety.org
Membership of 175, covering all aspects of crafts. Exhibitions in Aldeburgh in July/August and in Bury St Edmunds in November/December annually.

TAFTA (The Australian Forum for Textile Arts)

PO Box 38, The Gap, Australia Q4061
t + 61 7 3300 6491 f + 61 7 3300 2148
e tafta@uq.net.au
w www.ggcreations.com.au/tafta
Quarterly colour magazine 'Textile Fibre Forum'; two-week-long textile 'forum' workshop/conferences annually; networking; support; taking Australia to the world.

Textile Society

32 Tatton Road South, Heaton Moor, Stockport SK4 4LU
t 0161 432 0419
e 100416.2731@compuserve.com
w www.textilesociety.org.uk
The Textile Society is a registered charity which aims to unite all in the study of textile art, design and history. See also ad on p. 11.

William Morris Society

Kelmscott House, 26 Upper Mall, Hammersmith, London W6 9TA
t 020 8741 3735 f 020 8748 5207
e william.morris@care4free.net
w morrissociety.org
Promoting the life and work of William Morris.

Private Colleges and Workshop Organisers

Alison Victoria School of Sewing
The Ferrers Centre for Arts & Crafts,
Staunton Harold, Ashby-de-la-Zouch,
Leicestershire LE65 1RU
t 01332 865139 f 01530 835668
e alison@schoolofsewing.co.uk
w www.schoolofsewing.co.uk
*Workshops in dressmaking, tailoring and
corsetry. Beginners through to advanced
techniques.*

Art Van Go
The Studios, 1 Stevenage Road, Knebworth,
Hertfordshire SG3 6AN
t 01438 814946 f 01438 816267
e art@artvango.co.uk
w www.artvango.co.uk
*An extensive range of workshops held on the
premises using distinguished local and national
tutors. See also Art Galleries and Exhibitions;
Mail Order Suppliers (Art Materials; Dyes/Silk
Paints); Shops (Art Materials; Dyes/Silk
Paints); ad on inside front cover.*

Bowen House Embroidery and Textile Workshops
68 Huntingdon Road, York YO31 8RN
t 01904 338700
e valwoodyork@aol.com
w www.bowenhouse.co.uk
*Creative textile/embroidery courses in York for
beginners/experienced. Includes freehand
machine embroidery, fabric manipulation,
experimental applique, feltmaking.*

Cajobah Gallery
Contemporary Craft Gallery, 3 Hamilton
Square, Birkenhead, Wirral CH41 6AU
t 0151 647 9577 f 0151 647 9577
*Accredited City & Guilds offering weekend
course programme includes Embroidery,
Papercraft, Feltmaking. Also day courses in
a range of creative skills. See also Art and
Craft Centres.*

Creative Escapes
Ashdown, Hoden Lane, Cleeve Prior,
Nr Evesham WR11 8LH
t 0870 220 2820 f 01386 760401
e ttd@creativeescapes.co.uk
w www.creativeescapes.co.uk
Consult the experts for help with your textile event. Textile art and beading workshops are our speciality.

Creative Leisure
St Marks, Cautley, Sedbergh, Cumbria
LA10 5LZ
t 01539 620287 f 01539 621585
e st.marks@talk21.com
w www.saintmarks.uk.com
Victorian vicarage, ensuite accommodation, delicious Aga food, homely atmosphere, excellent studio facilities situated in Howgill Fells in Dales National Park.

Creative Needles (Chrissy Bristow)
1 Highbury Villas, Ash Green Road, Ash Green, Surrey GU12 6JF
t 01252 312326
e chrissy.bristow@virgin.net
w www.chrissybristow.co.uk
Chrissy Bristow and Hazel Everett teach both day and evening classes on beadwork and embroidery. The classes are held in Ash, Surrey, and cover all abilities. See also Beads, Beads, Beads; Textile Artists and Designers.

Dee Flanaghan - Embroidery Tutor
5 Hartside Close, Gamston, Notts NG2 6NW
t 0115 982 6951
e deeflanaghan@btconnect.com
Embroidery classes at Gamston Village Hall, alternate Tuesday afternoons. Day schools for machine-made cords, braids and tassels. Also basic quilting.

Hilltop
Windmill Cross, Canterbury Road, Lyminge, Folkestone, Kent CT18 8HD
t 01303 862617
e info@handspin.co.uk
w www.handspin.co.uk
Specialists in spinning, weaving and related textile craft supplies and tuition. Free mail order brochure. See also Mail Order Suppliers (Weaving/Spinning/Felt); Publications; Specialist Breaks; Textile Tours; Websites; ad on p. 47.

Inkberrow Design Centre
The Westall Centre, Holberrow Green, Nr Redditch B97 6JY
t 01386 793793 f 01386 793364
e Brenda@idcink.fsnet.co.uk
Private and school workshops in all aspects of Embroidery, Millinery, Fashion, Interior Design, Floristry, Vocational GCSE. Call for latest information. See also Adult and Further Education; Art and Craft Centres.

INtuition
The Woodlands, West Side, North Littleton, Evesham WR11 8QP
t 01386 832932 f 01386 832621
e judy.size@firenet.uk.com
Weekly classes, one-day workshops and summer schools in soft furnishings, upholstery, decorative sewing techniques - patchwork, quilting, appliqué, machine embroidery, etc.

Jan Wright/Sean Carey's Workshops with Pleasure
32 Berkeley Road, Coventry CV5 6NX
t 02476 679117 f 02476 679117
e michaelhawkins@tiscali.co.uk
Providing a unique, simple and inexpensive approach to dress pattern making and garment design. At workshops and postal courses, nationwide.

Masterclass at Bucklers Farm
85 Lexden Road, West Bergholt, Colchester, Essex CO6 3BW
t 01206 240568 f 01206 240568
e masterclass@aspects.net
Throughout the year, Masterclass offers a wide variety of courses in embroidery, textiles and related subjects for all levels.

Needle and Frame
45 S Park Victoria Drive #459, Milpitas, California 95035, USA
t +1 408 957 8742
e sandra@needleandframe.com
w needleandframe.com
Beading, needlework kits, beginners to advanced in traditional embroidery. Classes for EGA, ANG groups, around USA with Creative Arts and Textile Show.

Opus School of Textile Arts

20 Crown Street, Harrow on the Hill,
Middlesex HA2 0HR
t 020 8864 7283 **f** 020 8423 3001
e enquiries@opus-online.co.uk
w www.opus-online.co.uk
Opus offers a creative approach to textile study,
providing correspondence courses from beginners
to degree level and classes in London. See also
Distance Learning; Higher Education/Research
Centres; ad on p. 54.

Rowandean Embroidery

1 Richmond Drive, Duffield, Derbyshire
DE56 4AB
t 01773 550755 **f** 01773 550755
e ted@rowandean.com
w www.rowandean.com
We offer one-day workshops covering all aspects
of hand embroidery. Suitable for beginners and
the more experienced embroiderer alike.

Royal School of Needlework

Apartment 12a, Hampton Court Palace,
Hampton Court, Surrey KT8 9AU
t 020 8943 1432 **f** 020 8943 4910
e rnwork@intonet.co.uk
w www.royal-needlework.co.uk
Hand embroidery courses in various techniques
and suitable for all levels. Private commissions
undertaken. Specialist training on three-year
Apprenticeship Scheme.

Shilasdair Yarns

10 Carnach, Waternish, Isle of Skye IV55
8GL, Scotland
t 01470 592297 **f** 0870 135 1341
e eva@shilasdair-yarns.co.uk
f shilasdair-yarns.co.uk
Natural dyed and self-coloured yarns and
designer sweaters plus spinning and dyecraft
supplies and tuition on beautiful Isle of Skye. See
also ad on p. 39.

Snail Trail Handweavers

Penwenallt Farm, Cilgerran, Cardigan SA43 2TP
t 01239 841228 **f** 01239 841228
e martin@snail-trail.co.uk
w www.snail-trail.co.uk
Weaving, spinning and dyeing courses,
residential and non-residential. April to October,
suitable for beginners and experienced. Small
groups, maximum six.

Dianne Standen

104 High Street, Maryport, Cumbria
CA15 6EQ
t 01900 813378
w www.creative-textiles.co.uk
Felting, recycling textiles workshops. Own
studio but will travel summer to other locations.
'A' level/Textile students welcome - short
residential courses. See also Specialist Breaks and
Holidays; Textile Artists and Designers;
Websites.

Elza Tantcheva

The Limes, Tickenham Hill, Tickenham,
Clevedon, North Somerset BS21 6SW
t 01275 857845 **f** 01275 856094
e etan711@aol.com
Workshops, talks and demonstrations on
tapestry weaving, hand-felting and Procion dyes.
Talks on Bulgarian textiles. See also Textile
Artists and Designers.

Textile Daze

38 Marlborough Avenue, Bromsgrove,
Worcestershire B60 2PD
t 01527 877615
e artfuldaze@handbag.com
Specialist textile and embroidery workshops with
top name tutors from Britain, USA and Canada.

(The) Textile Restoration Studio

2 Talbot Road, Bowdon, Altrincham,
Cheshire WA14 3JD
t 0161 928 0020 **f** 0161 928 0020
e enquiries @textilerestoration.co.uk
w www.textilerestoration.co.uk
Specialist study days and residential weekend
courses on textile and ecclesiastical conservation
covering repair techniques, mounting, display
and storage. See also Antiques/Auctions/
Conservation.

Textile Workshops at Tavistock College

Cave Canem, King Street, Gunnislake,
Cornwall PL18 9JS
t 01822 833946
e victor@briggs607.fsnet.co.uk
Bringing top traditional and contemporary
tutors in all needlecrafts to the South West.

Rita Trefois
Lijnmolenstraat 52, 9040 Gent, Belgium
t +32 09 229 18 49 **f** +32 09 229 18 49
e rita.trefois@pandora.be
Trained in textile chemistry and decorative art,
batik artist and lecturer since mid-70s.
Promoting batik in lectures and workshops.

West Dean College
Chichester, West Sussex PO18 0QZ
t 01243 811301 **f** 01243 811343
e enquiries@westdean.org.uk
w www.westdean.org.uk
Short courses in textile media (embroidery,
stitch, painting, printing, dyeing, weaving, lace-
making and other techniques). Postgraduate
diplomas in tapestry weaving. See also Adult
and Further Education; Higher Education/
Research Centres; Textile Artists and Designers.

Wombourne School of Millinery
Mill Lane Farmhouse, Mill Lane,
Wombourne, Staffs WV5 0LE
t 01902 893683 **f** 01902 893683
e courses@hatblocks.co.uk
w www.hatblocks.co.uk
Offers a wide variety of courses from 1 to 5 days
on all aspects of millinery techniques. B&B list
available.

Private Colleges and Workshop Organisers by area

East Anglia
Masterclass at Bucklers Farm

Midlands
Alison Victoria School of Sewing
Dee Flanaghan - Embroidery Tutor
Inkberrow Design Centre
INtuition
Rowandean Embroidery
Textile Daze
Wombourne School of Millinery

North East
Bowen House Embroidery and Textile
   Workshops

North West
Cajobah Gallery
Creative Leisure
Dianne Standen
The Textile Restoration Studio

Scotland
Shilasdair Yarns

South Central
West Dean College

South East
Art Van Go
Creative Needles
Hilltop
Opus School of Textile Arts
Royal School of Needlework

South West
Elza Tantcheva
Textile Workshops at Tavistock College

Wales
Snail Trail Handweavers

UK
Creative Escapes
Jan Wright/Sean Carey's Workshops with
   Pleasure

Belgium
Rita Trefois

USA
Needle and Frame

Publications

Bead & Button
PO Box 1612, Waukesha, WI 53187-9950, USA
t +1 262 796 8776 X 421 **f** +1 262 796 1615
e customerservice@kalmbach.com
w www.beadandbutton.com
Email or visit the website for subscription information. Also available from bead sellers in the UK (find them in Beads, Beads, Beads).

Beadwork
Interweave Press Inc, 201 E Fourth Street, Loveland CO 80537-5655, USA
t +1 970 669 7672
e beadwork@interweave.com
w www.interweave.com
Email or visit the website for subscription information. Also available from bead sellers in the UK (find them in Beads, Beads, Beads).

Classic Stitches Magazine
80 Kingsway East, Dundee DD4 8SL
t 01382 223131 **f** 01382 452491
e editorial@classicstitches.com
w www.classicstitches.com
A magazine and website packed full of great stitching ideas, step-by-step techniques and information.

Crafts Beautiful
Castle House, 97 High Street, Colchester, Essex CO1 1TH
t 01206 505950 **f** 01206 505945
e martinlack@u.genie.co.uk
w www.crafts-beautiful.com
The UK's best selling craft magazine, written in a step-by-step project style with many textile-related features.

Crafts Magazine
44a Pentonville Road, London N1 9BY
t 020 7806 2542 **f** 020 7837 0858
e crafts@craftscouncil.org.uk
w www.craftscouncil.org.uk
The only magazine to explore and promote excellence across the whole range of crafts disciplines.

(The) Craftsman Magazine (incorporating FibreAction)
(PSB Design and Print Consultants Ltd)
PO Box 5, Driffield YO25 8JD
t 01377 255213 **f** 01377 255730
e info@craftsman-magazine.com
w www.craftsmanonline.co.uk
Monthly magazine for professional makers and designers, with 'FibreAction' 12-page section every quarter, February, May, August & November.

Cross Stitch Crazy
Origin Publishing Ltd, 14th Floor, Tower House, Bristol BS1 3BN
t 0117 927 9009 **f** 0117 934 9008
e catherine@cross-stitching.com
A fantastic magazine for cross stitchers, packed with great charts, stitching tips and expert advice.

Double Trouble Enterprises
233 Courthouse Road, Maidenhead SL6 6HF
t 01628 675699
w www.doubletrouble-ent.com
Jan Beaney and Jean Littlejohn have written a wide range of inspirational and informative booklets in full colour (see website).

Embroidery
Embroiderers' Guild, Apt 41 Hampton Court Palace, Hampton Court, Surrey KT8 9AU
t 020 8943 1229 **f** 020 8977 9882
e administrator@embroiderersguild.com
w www.embroiderersguild.com
Essential magazine for the professional, enthusiast, teacher, collector and historian.Features on contemporary textile art, history and social history of embroidery, ethnographic textiles, important collections. Exhibition reviews, books, news.

Fabrications - Patchwork and Quilting with Embroidery
21 High Street, Spalding, Lincs PE11 1TX
t 01775 722900 **f** 01775 713125
e house@gxn.co.uk
w www.grosvenor-publishing.co.uk
We publish bi-monthly. Available at all patchwork and quilting shows and high street newsagents.

GMC Publications Ltd
166 High Street, Lewes, East Sussex
BN7 1XU
t 01273 488005
Over 1000 craft titles including more than 150 books about knitting, crochet, dressmaking, embroidery and quilting. See ad on p. 95.

Hilltop
Windmill Cross, Canterbury Road, Lyminge, Folkestone, Kent CT18 8HD
t 01303 862617
e info@handspin.co.uk
w www.handspin.co.uk
Publishers of A4 laminates and booklets on textile craft related subjects. See also Mail Order Suppliers (Weaving/Spinning/Felt); Private Colleges and Workshop Organisers; Specialist Breaks; Textile Tours; Websites; ad on p. 47.

Maggie Grey's Workshop on the Web
7 Heath Farm Way, Ferndown, Dorset
BH22 8JR
t 01202 872429 **f** 01202 897211
e maggie@workshopontheweb.com
w www.workshopontheweb.com
Fancy a workshop with a top tutor such as Val Campbell-Harding, Ruth Issett or Maggie Grey? Online embroidery classes. See also Websites; ad on p. 98.

In a Spin
127A High Street, Uckfield, East Sussex
TN22 1EH
t 01825 764444
e joany46@aol.com
w www.spinning4ewe.co.uk
'In a Spin' is a quarterly publication for spinners/weavers and dyers everywhere. With articles, classified and diary, very useful.

Inspirations For Your Home
SPL Publishing, Berwick House, 8-10 Knoll Rise, Kent BR6 0PS
t 01689 887200 **f** 01689 896847
e inspirations@spl.publishing.co.uk
'Inspirations' offers readers a wealth of ideas and projects to help you make the home of your dreams.

Jane Greenoff's Cross Stitch
Future Publishing Ltd, Beauford Court, 30 Monmouth Street, Bath BA1 2BW
t 01225 442244 **f** 01225 446019
e debora.bradley@futurenet.co.uk
Bi-monthly magazine for cross stitchers of all abilities. Full of designs, big and small projects, competitions, news and more.

Jill Oxton's Cross Stitch & Beading
Jill Oxton Publications Pty Ltd, ACN 054 893 926, PO Box 283, Park Holme, South Australia 5043
t +61 8 8276 2722 **f** +61 8 8374 3494
e jaoxton@box.net.au
w www.jilloxtonxstitch.com
Beautiful photography, easy-to-read charts, clear instructions, helpful hints and imaginative making up ideas for your needlework.

Journal for Weavers, Spinners & Dyers
Bryn Eglwys, Pontygwyddel, Llanfair, Talhaiarn, Abergele LL22 9RB
t 01745 540360 **f** 01745 540412
e spunyarn@which.net
w www.wsd.org.uk
The Journal, published quarterly, is the only magazine produced in the UK specifically for weavers, spinners and dyers.

Machine Knitting News
PO Box 2730, Lewes BN8 4DQ
t 01273 400425 **f** 01273 400429
e chrispics@aol.com
Packed with modern patterns, expert tips, news and competitions. To order call 01273 488005. See ad on inside back cover.

(The) Marcan Handbook of Arts Organisations
Peter Marcan Publications, PO Box 3158, London SE1 4RA
t 020 7357 0368
Entries for over 2000 organisations, English, Welsh, Scottish, Irish, regional, international. Information sources in all areas of arts and culture.

Needlecraft

Future Publishing Ltd, Beauford Court,
30 Monmouth Street, Bath BA1 2BW
t 01225 442244 **f** 01225 446019
e needlecraft@futurenet.co.uk
*Monthly magazine packed with cross stitch,
embroidery, canvaswork, patchwork, quilting,
appliqué and many other needlework techniques.*

New Stitches/Cross Stitch Gallery

Well Oast, Brenley Lane, Faversham,
Kent ME13 9LY
t 01227 750215 **f** 01227 750813
e enquiries@ccpuk.co.uk
w www.creativecrafts.net
*Top-quality publications with worldwide
circulation. NS: cross stitch projects, Master
Classes, other techniques.CSG: mainly smaller
cross stitch designs.*

Patchwork & Quilting Magazine

Traplet Publications Ltd, Traplet House,
Severn Drive, Upton upon Severn, Worcs
WR8 0JL
t 01684 595300 **f** 01684 594586
e marketing@traplet.com
w www.traplet.com
*The essential magazine for all those interested in
the hobby of patchwork and quilting.*

Popular Crafts

Nexus Media, Azalea Drive, Swanley,
Kent BR8 8HU
t 01322 660070 **f** 01322 616319
e info@nexusmedia.com
w www.nexusonline.com
*Offers exciting projects, handy tips, the latest
news and events information.*

Popular Patchwork

Nexus House, Azalea Drive, Swanley,
Kent BR8 8HU
t 01322 660070 **f** 01322 616319
e info@nexusmedia.com
w www.nexusonline.com
*Monthly magazine that is essential reading for
today's quilter. Patchwork, quilting, appliqué,
designs, projects. Available on subscription and
at newsagents.*

Rag Rug News

The Rug Studio, 18 Elmcroft, Oxton,
Notts NG25 0SB
t 0115 965 5287/07752 772474 **f** 0115 965 5287
e cilla@jpcameron.fsnet.co.uk
w www.nowanowa.com/ragrugs
*This quarterly newsletter for rug makers
includes a list of teachers and workshops/courses,
rug schools, rug groups, exhibitions, suppliers.*

Rowan and Jaeger Handknits

Green Lane Mill, Holmfirth, W Yorks
HD9 2DX
t 01484 681881 **f** 01484 687920
e mail@knitrowan.com
w www.knitrowan.com
*The best in handknitting design with a range of
knitting magazines, beautiful yarns and knitting
courses nationwide. See also Adult and Further
Education; Mail Order Suppliers (Knitting/
Crochet); Websites.*

Ruth Bean Publishers

Victoria Farmhouse, Carlton, Bedford
MK43 7LP
t 01234 720356 **f** 01234 720590
e ruthbean@onetel.net.uk
*Publishers of both historical and practical books
on costume, embroidery, lacemaking and
weaving.*

Search Press Ltd

Wellwood, North Farm Road, Tunbridge
Wells, Kent TN2 3DR
t 01892 510850 **f** 01892 515903
e searchpress@searchpress.com
w www.searchpress.com
*Specialist in arts and crafts publications with a
wide variety of titles in creative textiles.*

Sewing with Butterick

Butterick Company Ltd, New Lane, Havant
PO9 2ND
t 023 9248 9773 **f** 023 9249 2769
e gail@butterick-vogue.co.uk
*'Hot Looks' from the High Street for fashion
sewers, home decoration enthusiasts and
needlecrafters of all ages and skill levels.*

Sewing with Butterick/Vogue Patterns - Weddings
Butterick Company Ltd, New Lane, Havant PO9 2ND
t 023 9248 9773 **f** 023 9249 2769
e gail@butterick-vogue.co.uk
The only bridal magazine for home sewers and professional dressmakers. Save up to 75% of the cost of similar shop-bought traditional and avant garde styles.

Sewing World
Traplet Publications Ltd, Traplet House, Severn Drive, Upton upon Severn, Worcs WR8 0JL
t 01684 595300 **f** 01684 594586
e sw@traplet.com
w www.traplet.com
Monthly magazine for sewing machine enthusiasts, packed with tips, techniques and features on sewing for home, fashion or fun.

Stitch with the Embroiderers Guild
Embroiderers' Guild, Apt 41 Hampton Court Palace, Hampton Court, Surrey KT8 9AU
t 020 8943 1229 **f** 020 8977 9882
e stitch.editor@talk21.com
w www.embroderersguild.com
Full colour, bi-monthly magazine which explores traditional embroidery techniques and creative contemporary ideas through how-to-do-it projects. Plus historical needlework, features, reviews, competitions.

Telos Art Publishing
PO Box 125, Winchester, Hants SO23 7UJ
t 01962 864546 **f** 01962 864727
e sales@telos.net
w www.telos.net
We offer high-quality books on textile art with excellent full-colour illustrations and highly informative text.

Textile Forum Magazine
Postbox 5944, D-30059 Hannover, Germany
t +49 511 817007 **f** +49 511 813108
e tfs@etn-net.org
w www.etn-net.org/tfs
Textile/fashion production/products in the arts, crafts and industry, textile heritage, education in textiles/fashion/costume, textile publications (books, magazines).

(The) Useful Booklet Company Ltd
PO Box 3294, Stratton-on-the-Fosse, Radstock BA3 4WL
Booklets for beginners. Our first booklet 'Daisy Chains' has 16 easy beadwork projects. Available by mail order £6.99 + 75p p&p.

Vogue Patterns Magazine
Butterick Company Ltd, New Lane, Havant PO9 2ND
t 023 9248 9773 **f** 023 9249 2769
e gail@butterick-vogue.co.uk
The only magazine offering sewing patterns straight from the catwalk collections of leading international designers.

Workbox Magazine
PO Box 25, Liskeard, Cornwall PL14 6XX
t 01579 340100 **f** 01579 340400
e workbox@ebony.co.uk
w www.ebony.co.uk
Informative and inspirational features on all aspects of needlecrafts for the student and enthusiast.

(The) World of Cross Stitching
Origin Publishing Ltd, 14th Floor, Tower House, Bristol BS1 3BN
t 0117 927 9009 **f** 0117 934 9008
w www.cross-stitching.com
Featuring designs from the UK's best designers, 'The World of Cross Stitching' is a must for all cross stitchers.

(The) World of Rag Rugs
Emlyn House, Quarry Ffinnant, Newcastle Emlyn, Carmarthenshire SA38 9HP
t 01239 711733
e WorldofRagRugs@wales02.fsnet.co.uk
International and national news and views. New quarterly newsletter out now!

Sewing Machine Makers/Parts/Service

Barnet Sewing Machines
53 Oakfield Close, Potters Bar, Hertfordshire
EN6 2BE
t 01707 665992 f 01707 663391
e sewingisfun@globlanet.co.uk
*New and reconditioned sewing machines,
servicing and repairs. Collection and delivery
arranged.*

C Thompson Machines Ltd
Patterson Street Blaydon, Haugh Ind Est,
Blaydon-on-Tyne NE21 5SD
t 0870 740 7552
e sales@cthompson.org.uk
w www.cthompson.org.uk
*C Thompson Machines for industrial sewing
machines. Toyota embroidery machines, software,
digitising, steam pressing, fusing and cutting
equipment. Rentals/sales.*

City Road Sewing Machine Service
175, Princess Road, Manchester M14 4RL
t 0161 226 2157
*Repair specialists, sewing machine sales,
industrial/domestic, any age repaired, new and
secondhand sold. Industrial machines for hire,
competitive rates.*

Connah Sewing Services
15 White Horse Street, Baldock, Herts
SG7 6QB
t 01462 892613 f 01462 892613
e connahsewing@aol.com
*Service, repairs and rentals. Most makes.
Agents for Brother sewing machines.*

Dave's Sewing Machine Repairs
12 Stump Cross, Boroughbridge, York, North
Yorkshire YO51 9HU
t 01423 322571
*Repairs to all makes and models. New and recon-
ditioned machine sales. Part exchange welcome.
All work guaranteed. Evening calls welcome.*

David Bridekirk
107 St Marks Road, Henley-on-Thames,
Oxfordshire RG9 1LP
t 01491 412666
*All makes of sewing machine serviced and
repaired. New and used sewing machines sold at
competitive prices.*

J Wishart
23 Edenaveys Crescent, Armagh BT60 1NT
t 028 3752 2601
*Specialists in domestic sewing machine sales,
service and repair for over 50 years.*

Jerry Fried Domestic & Co Ltd
Saltmeadows Rd, Gateshead, Tyne and Wear
NE8 3BQ
t 0191 490 1313 f 0191 490 1907
e sales@jerryfried.co.uk
w www.jerryfried.co.uk
*Distributor of industrial and Necchi household
sewing machines/steam irons with boilers/presses
plus 200,000 sewing machine parts and
accessories.*

M J Woods & Co
Unit 7d, Beckingham Business Park,
Tolleshunt Major, Maldon, Essex CM9 8LZ
t 01621 869863 f 01621 869864
e Bernina-East-Anglia@msn.com
*We specialise in Bernina sewing machiine sales,
service and accessories.*

Midland Motor Rewinds
Units 6 & 23, Hive Ind Est, Factory Road,
Hockley, Birmingham B18 5JU
t 0121 551 2323 f 0121 554 2295
e mmr@sewingmachines-uk.com
w www.sewingmachines-uk.com
*Sales and repairs to all types of industrial and
domestic sewing machines, steam press
equipment, motors.*

Sewing Machine Maintenance
Silchester Rd, Tadley, Hampshire RG26 3PY
t 0118 981 1200 f 0118 981 0197
e hireit@countryhire.com
*Any make of domestic sewing machine serviced
or repaired.*

Sewing Machine Repairs
40 Northgate Way, Terrington St Clement,
King's Lynn, Norfolk PE34 4LG
t 01553 828752
*Repairs and servicing to all makes of
sewing machine.*

A new challenge

After you have tried a couple of one-day workshops, and maybe a weekend course or two, you might be feeling in need of a new challenge. Perhaps a longer course in an art or craft subject so that you can really get your teeth into it?

The City & Guilds 7802 courses, in over a hundred subjects, are worth investigating. They are one-year courses, either taking place one day a week during term time, or for six or seven weekends per year at a residential college. This is the chance if you are a beginner at a subject to learn it from the bottom up, or if you have already got qualifications in a related skill, to study some aspect of it in more depth. Your fellow students will come from all sorts of backgrounds, and will have a number of different skills and experiences already, but the course will encompass all these and everyone will learn from each other. New friends, new opportunities, new ideas and new experiences will enrich your life in many ways.

You are likely to begin such a course by discovering what is going to be covered during the year, what materials you will need and what techniques you will learn, what skills you will touch on and what skills you will cover in more depth. You will be keeping notes and samples in a workbook, and these are often extremely interesting and beautiful, showing how your own ideas have developed. Your tutor will give you deadlines at intervals during the course when you should

have finished certain parts of it, and you will need to do some homework in order to achieve this. A good excuse not to clean out the cupboards or do the ironing.

On a craft course you will be making some finished pieces and probably showing these to your friends and family, and the general public, at an exhibition. The admiration and respect you gain will help you to become more confident, and you will find yourself encouraging others to go through the same enriching experience, gaining the same satisfaction as you have.

A year is not too long a period to commit yourself, and many students, after a 7802 course, have become course junkies, developing such a thirst for learning that they look around for another subject to study for a second year, and maybe a third one too.

Ask your local college for a brochure for the weekly courses, or go online to the Adult Residential College Association web site for the weekend courses. The url is aredu.org.uk, and you can do a search by area or subject.

Have a go, why not?

Valerie Campbell-Harding

Art Materials

Art Van Go

The Studios, 1 Stevenage Road, Knebworth,
Hertfordshire SG3 6AN
t 01438 814946 **f** 01438 816267
e art@artvango.co.uk
w www.artvango.co.uk
An exciting range of art and textile materials for surface and structural embellishment. Car-park. BR station 5 minutes walk. See also Art Galleries and Exhibitions; Mail Order Suppliers (Art Materials; Dyes/Silk Paints); Shops (Dyes/Silk Paints); Private Colleges and Workshop Organisers; ad on inside front cover.

ArtiSan's

9 Station Road, Settle, North Yorkshire
BD24 9AA
t 01729 825757
I stock artists' and craft materials. I now specialise in products for textile workers and embroiderers and offer mail order. See also Shops (Dyes/Silk Paints); ad on this page.

CRA

118 London Rd, St Albans, Herts AL1 1NX
t 01727 851555 **f** 01727 839331
e info@c-r-a.co.uk **w** www.c-r-a.co.uk
Paints for all fabrics/surfaces available from stock

Ceres Crafts

Lansdown Rd, Bude, Cornwall EX23 8BH
t 01288 354070
Retailing of art and craft materials. Winsor & Newton Premier Art Centre.

Dorrie Doodle

50 Bridge St, Aberdeen, Aberdeenshire
AB11 6JN
t 01224 212821 **f** 01224 212821
e dorriedood@aol.com
w dorriedoodle.co.uk
Unusual items of paper and things to cross-stitch over. Range of stamps, many with the stitcher in mind.

Dyes/Silk Paints

Art Van Go 🅣
The Studios, 1 Stevenage Road, Knebworth,
Hertfordshire SG3 6AN
t 01438 814946 f 01438 816267
e art@artvango.co.uk
w www.artvango.co.uk
*Silk & velvet by the metre, dyes, silk paints and
accessories. Car-park. BR station 5 minutes walk.
See also Art Galleries and Exhibitions; Mail
Order Suppliers (Art Materials; Dyes/Silk
Paints); Private Colleges and Workshop
Organisers; Shops (Art Materials); ad on inside
front cover.*

ArtiSan's
9 Station Road, Settle, North Yorkshire
BD24 9AA
t 01729 825757
*I stock artists' and craft materials. I now
specialise in products for textile workers and
embroiderers and offer mail order. See also Shops
(Art Materials); ad on p. 65.*

Rainbow Silks 🅣
6 Wheelers Yard, Great Missenden, Bucks
HP16 0AL
t 01494 862111 f 01494 862651
e caroline@rainbowsilks.co.uk
w www.rainbowsilks.co.uk
*Products for textile decoration and silk painting,
available by mail order/showroom. Creative
classes in our new studio – ask for details.*

Embroidery

Crown Needlework
115 High Street, Hungerford, Berkshire
RG17 0LU
t 01488 684011
*Thread specialist - Appletons, Anchor, DMC,
Paterna, Madeira, Caron, Kreinik: crochet, lace,
goldwork, machine embroidery. Embroidery
fabrics cut to your requirements.*

News flash
Many of you will have been upset by the sad news of
the closure of the Needlework Centre at Longleat in
July 2002. However, as we were going to press we
heard that Pam Cooper of Longleat is going to be
running workshops for From Debbie Cripps at their
Frome shop and studio. An extensive programme is
planned. Call 01373 454448 for details.

From Debbie Cripps 🅣
8 Christchurch Street West, Frome, Somerset
BA11 1EQ
t 01373 454448
e debbie@debbiecripps.co.uk
w www.debbiecripps.co.uk
*Celebrated designer Debbie Cripps presents her
exclusive range of needlework kits and a selection
of embellishments, craft products and gift items.*

Jenny Scott's Creative Embroidery 🅣
The Old Post Office, 39 Duke Street, Settle,
North Yorkshire BD24 9DJ
t 01729 824298 f 01729 824298
e jennyscott@amserve.com
*Creative and traditional workshops, experimental
packs, Elizabeth Bradley, Beverley Stitchery kits
and much more. Collectors' teddy bears, gifts,
mail order.*

Variegations
Rose Cottage, Harper Royd Lane, Norland,
Halifax HX6 3QQ
t 01422 832411
e variegat@globalnet.co.uk
w www.variegations.com
*Variegations Textile Art Centre, located in
Sowerby Bridge, is a paradise for textile artists.
Ring for a map and opening times. See also Mail
Order Suppliers (Embroidery).*

Fabrics

AMS Fabrics
7 Maurice Rd Ind Est, Wallsend, Tyne and
Wear NE28 6BY
t 0191 263 4095 f 0191 263 4095
*An Aladdin's Cave for the dressmaker. If we
don't have it you don't need it!*

(The) Bankrupt Shop Ltd
27-29 Stafford St, Liverpool, Merseyside
L3 8LX
t 0151 207 0531 f 0151 207 1880
e bankrupy@aol.com
w www.bankrupt-shop.com
*Upholstery and curtain fabric specialists with the
unique price of £2.90 per metre for all fabric.*

Blanshard Fabrics
21 Wallingford St, Wantage, Oxfordshire
OX12 8AU
t 01235 762465 **f** 01235 762465
A long-established family-run shop. Offering a wide range of dress fabrics, haberdashery, patterns, curtain fabrics, linings and cross-stitch.

Broadwick Silks Ltd
9-11 Broadwick St, London W1F 0DB
t 020 7734 3320
Broadwick Silks has a huge range of exquisite bridal, theatrical, dance and stunning special occasion fabrics from around the world.

C & H Fabrics Ltd
Stone House, 21-23 Church Rd, Tunbridge Wells, Kent TN1 1LT
t 01892 773600 **f** 01892 773621
e candh@candh.demon.co.uk
w www.candh.fabrics.co.uk
Seven stores in South East: Brighton, Chichester, Tunbridge Wells, Winchester, Eastbourne, Canterbury, Maidstone.

Cloth Market of Stamford
5 Stamford Walk, Stamford, Lincs PE9 2JE
t 01780 753409
High-quality furnishings and fabrics at reduced prices.

(The) Cloth Shop
42 Bridge St, Taunton, Somerset TA1 1UD
t 01823 253469
Established 30 years. Dress fabrics and home furnishings.

(The) Cloth Shop
7 Queen St, Seaton, Devon EX12 2NY
t 01297 21239
Established 30 years. Dress fabrics and home furnishings.

(The) Cloth Store
40 Queens Square, Crawley, West Sussex RH10 1HA
t 01293 560943
e theclothstore@aol.com
w www.clothstore.co.uk
Fashion & furnishing fabric. Haberdashery, craft, products, patterns, sewing machines, making-up service, Coats, DMC, Dylon, Velcro, classes.

(The) Cotton Mills
Peoples Palace, Pydar St, Truro, Cornwall TR1 2AZ
t 01872 278545 **f** 01872 263918
e cottonmills@amserve.net
A wide range of furnishing fabrics for your home.

(The) Curtain House
14 Gage Street, Lancaster LA1 1UH
t 01524 66931
w www.curtainhouse.co.uk
Suppliers of curtain and upholstery fabrics to the domestic and commercial customer. Design and make-up service provided.

curtainfabricsLtd.co.uk
50-52 Commercial Rd, Lower Parkstone, Poole, Dorset BH14 0JT
t 01202 740459 **f** 01202 723933
e curtainfabrics@aol.com
w curtainfabricsLtd.co.uk
Over the years we have built up a fine reputation as curtain fabric stockists and curtain makers.

Ebonique Designs
33 Victoria Street, Wolverhampton WV1 3PW
t 01902 827958 **f** 01902 827958
e ptamkennedy@aol.com
w www.eboniquedesigns.com
Importers of paintings, carvings, batiks, chess sets, furniture and textiles (ready-made clothing or fabric by the yard) from Africa.

Esberger Fabrics
Unit 64, Market Place, Crystal Peaks, Sheffield, South Yorkshire S1 2GH
t 0114 247 2287 **f** 01909 772296
Stockists of dress fabric, bridal, curtaining, voiles, haberdashery, patterns, cross-stitch, direct from mills and designers. Known for our low prices.

Esberger Fabrics
Unit 33 Market Hall, Low Pavement, Chesterfield, Derbyshire S40 1AR
t 01246 201330
Stockists dress fabric, bridal, curtaining, voiles and organzas. All major pattern companies, direct from mils and designers at lowest prices.

Essex Fabric Warehouse
Unit 2, Sainsburys Homebase, London Rd,
Vange, Basildon, Essex SS16 4PR
t 01268 552224 **f** 01268 556352
e jeanparker@essexfabricwarehouse.co.uk
*Over 6000 rolls of fabric to chose from for
curtains and upholstery. Also ready-mades, nets,
bedding, cushions, etc.*

(The) Fabric Company
10 Sussex St, Cambridge, Cambridgeshire
CB1 1PA
t 01223 461449 **f** 01223 366 816
e sales@fabric-company.co.uk
w www.fabric-company.co.uk
*Dress fabrics, bridal, party, haberdashery,
Aladdin's cave of fabrics.*

Fabric Magic
Station Approach, Trowbridge, Wiltshire
BA14 8HW
t 01225 768833
e fabricmagic@amserve.net
*Wide range of fabrics and haberdashery.
Workshops and mail order catalogue. Rowan
wools and patterns. Ring for details. Customer
parking.*

Fabric Warehouse
North St, King's Lynn, Norfolk PE30 1QW
t 01553 660491 **f** 01553 660645
*Soft furnishing fabrics on the roll and to order,
haberdashery, tracks and poles, nets, etc.
Personal service at discount prices.*

Fabric Warehouse
5-9 King St, Southport, Merseyside PR8 1LB
t 01704 537433 **f** 01704 545076
*Soft furnishing and curtain fabrics.
Haberdashery, accessories for upholstery.*

Greyhouse Fabrics
Halifax House, Mansfield Rd, Farnsfield,
Newark, Nottinghamshire NG22 8HF
t 01623 882124
*Beautiful soft furnishing fabrics. Made to order
service for curtains, blinds, etc.*

Hadson Exclusive Fabrics
197, Baker St, London NW1 6UY
t 020 7486 6696 **f** 020 7486 6626
e had@hadson.com
w www.hadson.com
*For exquisite, exclusive, elegant fabrics and saris,
scarves and shawls.*

Hangzhou Silks
3 Station Approach, Stoneleigh, Epsom,
Surrey KT19 0QZ
t 020 8393 1888 **f** 020 8393 4888
e hangzhousilks@hotmail.com
*Quality silk fabrics are always in stock at
competitive prices, no minimum quantities, next
day delivery for mail order.*

Hansson Silks
1st Floor, 108 Woodbridge Road, Guildford,
Surrey GU1 4PY
t 01483 451625 **f** 01483 451602
e sales@hansson-silks.co.uk
w www.hansson-silks.co.uk
*Silks for all needs. Bridal, soft furnishings,
hobbies, painting. Ball gowns, day wear, silk
embroideries, brocades for waistcoats.*

Hellerslea Fabrics
5 Lugley St, Newport, Isle of Wight
PO30 5HD
t 01983 526104 **f** 01983 527736
e berylhobbs@btconnect.com
w www.hellersleafabrics.co.uk
*Est. 1968 two-floor warehouse selling curtain
and dress fabric, knitting wool, haberdashery,
tapestries, run by mother and son Beryl
and Barry.*

Hotch Potch
45a High St, Haverfordwest, Dyfed
SA61 2BN
t 01437 760971
*Large remnant store. Specialises in dress, fancy
dress, disco dancing fabrics. Beads/trimmings.
Indian cotton upholstery. Loads of mess!*

House of Sandersons
139 Dudley Road, Brierley Hill,
West Midlands DY5 1HD
t 01384 70022 **f** 01384 70022
*Soft furnishing fabrics and drapes, tassels
and tiebacks.*

In-Fabrics
12 Old Bridge, Haverfordwest, Dyfed
SA61 2ET
t 01437 769164 **f** 01646 690282
e glynisrichards@supanet.com
w www.in-fabrics.gbr.cc
Specialists in quality warehouse clearance fabrics. 1000s of rolls in stock at unbeatable prices.

Jai Sareetex
94 Belgrave Road, Leicester LE4 5AT
t 0116 253 0484
Colourful range of fabrics. Sarees, silk fabrics, polyesters imported from Japan and India.

Jenkins Sewing Centre
302 Stanley Rd, Bootle, Merseyside L20 3ET
t 0151 944 2752 **f** 0151 9442752
Retail, dress, bridal and evening-wear fabrics, haberdashery and accessories. Also sewing machine sales, service and repairs.

Joan Weir Fabrics
31-33 Church St, Atherton, Manchester
M46 9DE
t 01942 877865
Fabrics, sewing patterns, buttons and all your haberdashery needs.

June Fabrics
32a King St, Blackpool, Lancashire FY1 3DL
t 01253 626705
All sorts of fabrics at low prices. Dress fabrics, curtain fabrics. Small amount of haberdashery.

Just Sew Fabrics
1a Seaford St, Kilmarnock, Ayrshire
KA1 2BZ
t 01563 527188
Bridal, formal & fancy dress fabrics, haberdashery, patterns, craft and favour-making materials, curtain fabrics & make-up service.

Kisko Fabrics (UK)
Kisko House, Cobden St, Leicester LE1 2LB
t 0116 262 0569
Largest range of quilting fabrics/accessories/fat quarters in the UK sold through the 'Fabric Guild UK'. £5 life membership.

Knickerbean Ltd
11 Holywell Hill, St Albans, Hertfordshire
AL1 1EZ
t 01727 866662 **f** 01727 866453
Fabulous selection of home fabrics in stock, many exclusively imported from Italy, France, USA, Spain, Belgium and the Far East.

Also at

5 Walcot Street, Bath, Avon BA1 5BN
t 01225 445741 **f** 01225 448862

4 Out Northgate Street, Bury St Edmunds,
Suffolk IP33 1JQ
t 01284 704055 **f** 01284 701647

8 Bartholomew Street, Newbury, Berkshire
RG14 5LL
t 01635 529016 **f** 01635 528636

Lili Fabrics
8 Laurie Walk, Romford, Essex RM1 3RT
t 01708 721184
An established business specialising in bridal, evening wear and theatrical costume fabrics. Also an extensive selection of exquisite voiles.

Louanne Fabrics
56/61 Market Hall, Arndale Centre, Luton,
Bedfordshire LU2 2TB
t 01582 736488
Dress fabrics - skirt, wedding, fleece, jerseys, denims, printed & plain cottons, tartans, crepe de chines, plain and patterned polyester jerseys.

McNeely Discount Soft Furnishings
18 Athorpe Grove, Dinnington, Sheffield
S25 2LD
t 01909 562916
e shaun@mcneely.fslife.co.uk
Supplier of quality fabrics at vastly reduced prices, including cotton prints, jacquards and velvets. Large selection of remnants also available.

Mears Ghyll Fabrics
Brookhouse Stores, Brookhouse, Lancaster
LA2 9JP
t 01524 770437
e Paulinehall@mearsghyll.fsbusiness.co.uk
w www.mearsghyll.co.uk
*Exclusive Swiss fabrics. One-day sewing
workshops and weekly classes. Stockists of bridal
fabrics, accessories. Wedding dresses designed to
commission.*

Michael's Bridal Fabrics (Wholesale) Ltd
Unit F15, Northfleet Ind Est, Lower Road,
Northfleet, Gravesend, Kent DA11 9SW
t 01322 380480/380568 f 01322 380680
e mbristow10@aol.com
w www.michaelsbridalfabrics.com
*We offer a wide range of fabrics suitable for all
the wedding party, including groom and mother
of the bride.*

Pats
81 Main St, West Kilbride, Ayrshire KA23 9AP
t 01294 822198
*We sell curtain, dress and voile fabrics. Curtain-
making service, dress alterations, dry cleaning,
wool and knitting patterns.*

R H Sands & Sons
52 Queen St, Maidenhead, Berkshire SL6 1HY
t 01628 624706 f 01628 415018
*Specialist furniture shop selling upholstery and
curtain fabrics, curtain making service and
upholstery available. Traditional house furnishers.*

Redwood Fabrics
Unit 2, Meadow Lane Trading Est, Meadow
Lane, Nottingham NG2 3HD
t 0115 985 2255 f 0115 985 2855
e amanda@redwood.joy-inter.net
w www.redwood-fabrics.com
*Import and export fabric merchants. Fashion and
furnishing fabrics. Wholesale and retail.
Commission agents also. See also Shops (Soft
Furnishing).*

Saffron
21 Bond St, Brighton, East Sussex BN1 1RD
t 01273 694919 f 01273 672859
e saffron@21bondst.freeserve.co.uk
*Supplying cotton and silk hand-woven textiles
with soft furnishing items, manufactured in
Southern India under fair trade.*

Sew Elegant
186b West St, Fareham, Hampshire
PO16 0HP
t 01329 220325 f 01329 220325
*Large selection of patchwork and quilting fabrics.
Also bridal and dress fabrics.*

Sew Fantastic
107 Essex Road, London N1 2SL
t 020 7226 2725
Fashion fabrics and haberdashery.

(The) Sewing Box
6 Village Walks, Queensway,
Poulton-le-Fylde, Lancashire FY6 7UR
t 01253 891748
*Curtain, craft and dress fabrics. Also thousands
of haberdashery items. Curtain accessories, fat
quarters, cushion panels, etc.*

(The) Skep
Springfield Commercial Centre, Bagley
Lane, Farsley, Pudsey, West Yorkshire
LS28 5LY
t 0113 255 6769
e robert@the-skep.co.uk
w www.the-skep.co.uk
*Fabrics and fancy yarns. All-wool cloth for
skirts/dresses/jackets. 100% cotton fabric for
patchwork. We offer mail order services.*

Tahim Drapers
388-394 Foleshill Rd, Coventry CV6 5AN
t 02476 685702
*Largest fabric showroom in the Midlands offering
fabrics from all over the world. Bridal,
dancewear, dressmaking, home furnishing and
much, much more.*

Textile Traders
37 High Street, Bishop's Castle, Shropshire
SY9 5BE
t 01588 638712 f 01588 638712
e enquiries@textiletechniques.co.uk
w www.textiletechniques.co.uk
*Specialists in fine hand-made textiles from
around the world - especially weaving, embroideries and batik equipment. Mail order service.
Talks and workshops.*

Warris Vianni & Co 🕐

85 Golborne Road, London W10 5NL
t 020 8964 0069
Specialist shop. Glamorous Indian fabrics. Good-quality basics: chenille, linen, cotton, organza, muslin, etc.

Framers/Frame Suppliers

(The) Frame Workshop

62 Broad Street, Hanley, Stoke-on-Trent, Staffs ST1 4EU
t 01782 286730 **f** 01782 286730
Framing needleworks and textiles is our speciality. Expert and individual service. Also DMC main agents stocking all needlecraft products.

General Needlecraft

Alison's

63 Hatfield Road, St Albans, Hertfordshire AL1 4JE
t 01727 833738 **f** 01727 848545
DMC centre. Embroidery silks, tapestry wools, kits and canvases. Cross-stitch kits. Knitting wools and patterns. Haberdashery.

Anne & Paul's Feltham Woolshop

8, Parkfield Parade, High Street, Feltham, Middlesex TW13 4HJ
t 020 8893 7779
w www.felthamwoolshop.co.uk
For all your knitting, sewing and needlecraft needs at budget prices. Stockists of the Pony Total Knitting System.

Artefacts of Whitby 🕐

159 Church St, Whitby, North Yorkshire YO22 4AS
t 01947 820682 **f** 01947 820682
e amanda.artefacts@btinternet.com
Specialist hand needlework/craft gallery. Unusual threads, fabrics and gifts. We share your passion for needlework.

Arts & Crafts Studio

St Michaels Row, Grosvenor Shopping Centre, Chester CH1 1EF
t 01244 324900 **f** 01244 329993
e artycraft@lineone.net.uk
w arts-and-crafts-studio.co.uk
Fabrics, threads, charms, beads, kits, charts, ribbons, dyes, buttons, lamps, stamps, crafts, rugmaking, crochet, books, paints, silk, service.

Auntie Pat's Place 🕐

222 Monton Road, Monton Green, Eccles, Manchester M30 9LJ
t 0161 789 3306 **f** 0161 789 3306
Wools. Extensive colour range - 2 ply to double chunky. Thousands of patterns. Crochet, embroidery, haberdashery, helpful, experienced staff.

(The) Ball of Wool

47 High St, Chipping Sodbury, Bristol, Avon BS37 6BA
t 01454 313216 **f** 01454 313216
Lots of haberdashery. Güttermanm, Sylko, large range of ribbons. DMC threads/kits. Dressmaking patterns. Large selection of baby knitting yarn.

Bears & Stitches

4 Cumberland St, Woodbridge, Suffolk IP12 4AB
t 01394 388999 **f** 01394 388999
Supplies for all kinds of embroidery and needlework.

Branch Drapers House

Drapers House, 71 Connaught Avenue, Frinton-on-Sea, Essex CO13 9PP
t 01255 674456
e sewbranch@aol.com
w www.sewmuchmore.co.uk
The store with sew much more.

Burford Needlecraft 🕐

117 High Street, Burford, Oxfordshire OX18 4RG
t 01993 822136 **f** 01993 824740
e rbx20@dial.pipex.com
w www.needlework.co.uk
In stock: knitting, haberdashery, 1000s of charts, needlework kits, threads and fabrics, lamps, stools, firescreens, etc. Mail order. Classes available.

Buttons and Bows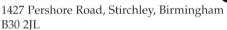
High Street, Castle Acre, King's Lynn,
Norfolk PE32 2BQ
t 01760 755387
*Appleton, Anchor, DMC, cotton fabrics
including theme collections - Christmas,
landscape, oriental, mythical birds, etc.*

Camelot Crafts
29 Station Terrace, Radcliffe on Trent,
Nottingham NG12 2AH
t 0115 933 5217
*DMC main agent, specialist threads, accessories,
beads, haberdashery, card making, glass paints
and more. Programme of classes/workshops.*

Canny Crafts
70 High St, Banchory, Kincardineshire AB31 5SS
t 01330 824979 **f** 01330 824979
e cannycrafts@hotmail.com
w www.cannycrafts.co.uk
*Award-winning needlework specialist.
Patchwork fabrics/accessories, tapestries,
cross-stitch, embroidery, threads, rubber
stamping, general crafts, haberdashery,
sewing machines, gifts.*

Choice
18 Pickford Lane, Bexleyheath, Kent DA7 4QW
t 020 8303 8762
e info@choice-uk.com
w www.choice-uk.com
*DMC main agent. Stockists for Heritage,
Dimensions, Sunset, Fabric Flair, Lanarie,
Derwentwater, Framecraft, etc. Sirdar and
Wendy wool and patterns.*

Cooper & Baumber
29 Market St, Gainsborough, Lincolnshire
DN21 2BE
t 01427 612946
*DMC main agent. Knitting wools - Sirdar,
Patons, Robin. Picture framing service.
Established 1907.*

Country Crafts
2 High St, Headley, Bordon, Hampshire
GU35 8PP
t 01428 714348
e pcpcrafts@supernet.com
*Country Crafts of Headley for all your knitting,
needlecraft and haberdashery requirements.
Friendly service, open Mon-Sat 9-5.*

Country Fabrics
Unit 2, Heart of the Country Craft Village,
London Rd, Swinfen, Lichfield WS14 9QR
t 01543 481989
*Craft and soft furnishing fabrics, haberdashery,
beads, design and making-up service.*

(The) Craft Centre
31 Palace Avenue, Paignton, Devon
TQ3 3EQ
t 01803 663607
*We carry all general craft material. Specialising
in needlework, cross-stitch and tapestry,
patchwork and quilting. Mail order available.*

Craftmill
98 Church Rd, Stockton-on-Tees, Cleveland
TS18 1TW
t 01642 351008 **f** 01642 351008
*Stockists of DMC and Anchor threads. 100s of
cross-stitch kits, Mill Hill beads, Kreinek, and all
your needlework needs.*

Crafts 'n' Sew On
1427 Pershore Road, Stirchley, Birmingham
B30 2JL
t 0121 433 3855
e craftsnsewon@btinternet.com
*Specialist needlecraft shop. Cross stitch,
canvaswork, embroidery, fabrics, accessories and
wide range of threads. Anchor and DMC main
agent.*

(The) Crafty Patch
3 South St, Bourne, Lincolnshire PE10 9LY
t 01778 422666
e magilloyd@thecraftypatch.fsnet.co.uk
w www.thecraftypatch.co.uk
*For all your crafty needs. Knitting, crochet and
all types of needlework. Many craft materials
stocked. Mail order welcome.*

Crazy Cross Stitcher
56 Regent St, Shanklin, Isle of Wight PO37 7AE
t 01983 866884 **f** 01983 866884
e alan@osmond.fsnet.co.uk
*Mail order available. Cross stitch, embroidery,
tapestry, DMC and Anchor main agent.*

Creative Crafts
11 The Square, Winchester, Hants SO23 9ES
t 01962 856266
e sales@creativecrafts.co.uk
w www.creativecrafts.co.uk
Full range of art and craft materials in stock.
Everything available by post or see website.

Cross Stitch Corner
Gillygate, Pontefract, W Yorkshire WF8 1PH
t 01977 602293
e sales@crossstitchcorner.co.uk
w www.crossstitchcorner.co.uk
Cross Stitch Corner specialises in cross stitch
embroidery products but other types of needle-
work can be obtained at customers' requests.

Don't Tell Mother
4 Regent Rd, Lowestoft, Suffolk NR32 1PA
t 01502 512555 **e** pemshore@hotmail.com
Stockists of Anchor and DMC stranded cotton,
fabrics, metallics, cross-stitch kits too numerous
to mention, cross-stitch publications, Craftime.

(The) Embroidery Shop
7 Market St, Tenbury Wells, Worcs WR15 8BH
t 01584 810906
Suppliers of DMC and Paterna threads. Many
cross-stitch and tapestry kits available. Silk
painting workshops and talks given.

Evangelines
58-61 St Nicholas Market, St Nicholas St,
Bristol BS1 1LJ
t 0117 925 7170 **f** 0117 970 2604
Cross stitch, tapestry, beads, ribbons, laces,
candlemaking, lacemaking, cards, peel offs,
flowers and much more. Postal service also.

Fabric Barn
Unit 2, Heart of the Country Craft Village,
London Rd, Swinfen, Lichfield WS14 9QR
t 01564 784764 **f** 01564 785912
Craft and soft furnishing fabrics, haberdashery.

Fantastic Fibres
49 Castle St, Thetford, Norfolk IP24 2DL
t 01842 752222
e terri.brown@lineone.net
w www.fantasticfibres.net
DMC embroidery and tapestry threads. Also
quilting, pergamano and rubber stamps supplies.
Free parking. Closed Mondays. Mail order
catalogue available.

Forge Mill Needle Museum
Needle Mill Lane, Riverside, Redditch,
Worcestershire B98 8HY
t 01527 62509 **f** 01527 66721
e museum@redditchbc.gov.uk
w www.redditchbc.gov.uk
Specialist in unusual machine and hand-sewing
needles, including curved needles. Museum shop
and mail order. See also Art Galleries and
Exhibitions; Museums.

Fourmark Art & Craft Centre
Bayshill Lodge, Montpellier St, Cheltenham,
Gloucestershire GL50 1SY
t 01242 231515 **f** 01242 231515
Stockist of DMC and Güttermann threads.
Comprehensive range of artists' materials, gener-
al crafts and graphic supplies.

Hemsleys
46 Steep Hill, Lincoln LN2 1LU
t 01522 514880
One of Britain's leading needlecraft shops
specialising in cross-stitch, tapestry, embroidery
and patchwork and quilting.

Hobby's
124 Darwen St, Blackburn, Lancashire BB2 2AJ
t 01254 56563 **f** 01254 670108
e info@hobkirk.co.uk
w www.hobkirk.co.uk
DMC main agents, Daylight premier stockist,
rubber stamping, Mill Hill beads, haberdashery,
sewing machines & accessories, pergamano, glass
paints, workshops.

Hobkirks Sewing Centres
119 Yorkshire St, Rochdale, Lancashire OL16 1DS
t 01706 647651 **f** 01706 647651
e info@hobkirk.co.uk
w www.hobkirk.co.uk
Stockists of sewing machines/accessories,
haberdashery, needlecraft specialist, DMC,
Lenarte, Derwent Water, Mouseloft Heritage,
Solo, framing service, Daylight stockist.

JEM's Sewing and Needlework Centre
19 Sun Street, Canterbury, Kent CT1 2HX
t 01227 457723 **f** 01227 456016
e info@jems-sewing.co.uk
w www.jems-sewing.co.uk
Sewing machines, overlockers, craft fabrics, cross-
stitch, tapestry, embroidery, beads, frames, classes.

Just Sew   **t**

Poets Walk, Penrith, Cumbria CA11 7HJ
t 01768 866791
*Inspiring fabric/haberdashery shop to help your
creativity.*

Just Sew

20 High St, Northwood, Middlesex HA6 1BN
t 01923 822042
e stephenwlee@btinternet.com
*We're only a small shop but carry a good range
of dress and craft fabrics, haberdashery items and
craft kits.*

K Fabrics

9a Church Walk, Trowbridge, Wiltshire
BA14 8DX
t 01225 766452
*Dress fabrics and patterns. Wool and patterns.
Making and alteration. Curtain fabric to order.*

Kay Krafts

3 Chapel Lane, Bingley, West Yorkshire
BD16 2NG
t 01274 511820
*Haberdashery. Materials and kits for cross stitch,
tapestry and embroidery. Craft materials. Card
making. Beads. Picture framing.
Mail order service.*

Knickers n' Lace

28 Onslow Rd, Layton, Blackpool FY3 7DF
t 01253 394008
*We stock knitting wool and patterns; sewing and
embroidery needs; threads; linings; lace; masks;
feathers; beads; also hosiery and underwear.*

Knitters Corner

26 Railway Approach, East Grinstead,
West Sussex RH19 1BP
t 01342 322480
*Knitting wools. Tapestry and cross-stitch kits.
Anchor silks and wools. Haberdashery, ribbons
and buttons.*

Knitting & Sewing Centre   **t**

28 Duke Street, Whitehaven, Cumbria
CA28 7EU
t 01946 63091
*From corset laces to the latest in sewing machines.
An Aladdin's cave for the needleworker.*

Lady Sew & Sew   **t**

Institute Rd (off High St), Marlow,
Buckinghamshire SL7 1BN
t 01628 890532 **f** 01491 577585
e info@ladysewandsew.co.uk
w www.ladysewandsew.co.uk
*Patchwork and quilting, wedding and evening
dress fabrics. Knitting yarns, cross stitch,
tapestries, haberdashery, curtaining, fleece and
fur. Mail order.*

Laurel Crafts   **t**

6 Springhill Lane, Penn, Wolverhampton
WV4 4SH
t 01902 330159 **f** 01902 330159
e michael019@btclick.com
w www.laurelcrafts.co.uk
*Craft supplies, one-day workshops, short courses,
craft holidays (non-tutored weeks or tutored
weekends), weekly classes, etc.*

Little Stitches   **t**

11, The Square, Aberfeldy, Perthshire
PH15 2DD
t 01887 829862 **f** 01887 829862
e littlestitches@lineone.net
*Small compact shop selling tapestries,
embroideries and card-making materials. Small
amount of haberdashery and patchwork fabrics.*

Maesteg Knitting Crafts

Bowrington Arcade, Neath Road, Maesteg,
Mid Glamorgan CF34 9EE
t 01656 730105
e mary@mkcrafts.fsnet.co.uk
*Together with a good selection of yarns, buttons,
embroidery and tapestry threads, kits and haberdashery, we also stock Welsh souvenirs*

Marion's Needlecraft & Miniatures

10, Oldgate, Morpeth, Northumberland
NE61 1LX
t 01670 512020
w www.marionsneedlecraftandminiatures.gbr.cc
*All your requirements for cross-stitch, tapestry,
embroidery and quilting from all leading
suppliers. Mail order customers welcome.*

Marion's Patchworks (t)

29 St Helens Rd, Swansea SA1 4AP
t 01792 470300 **f** 01792 470300
e marion.patchworks@zoom.co.uk
Patchwork, quilting and needlecraft supplies.
Books, Australian magazines, workshops and
classes.

Meynells Ltd (t)

2 Southfield Rd, Middlesbrough, Cleveland
TS1 3BZ
t 01642 247863 **f** 01642 247863
e sales@meynells.co.uk
w www.meynells.co.uk
Sewing and knitting machine sales and repairs.
Stockist of fabrics, haberdashery, knitting yarns,
rug kits, DMC and Craft Collection.

Needle & Thread (t)

80 High Street, Horsell, Woking, Surrey
GU21 4SZ
t 01483 760059
Cross-stitch and tapestry kits, embroidery
threads, patchwork and quilting supplies. Weekly
classes and one-day workshops in patchwork,
embroidery.

(The) Needleworker

7 Vine Street, Evesham WR11 4RE
t 01386 765844
For crafts, DMC & Anchor threads, haberdashery,
dress & craft patterns, fabrics, sewing machines
sales and servicing, sewing machine parts.

Newnham Court Crafts

Newnham Court Shopping Village, Bearsted
Road, Maidstone, Kent ME14 5LH
t 01622 630886 **f** 01622 630886
e newnham-court.crafts@virgin.net
w www.newnhamcourtcrafts.co.uk
A wide range of needlecraft goods; art and crafts
materials; card making; dolls' houses and
miniatures.

Nifty Needles

56, High St, Linlithgow, West Lothian
EH49 7AQ
t 01506 670435
e niftyneedles_linlithgow@hotmail.com
Everything stocked for cross stitch, embroidery,
tapestry, knitting, crochet. Stef Francis, Oliver
Twists, DMC, Anchor, Venus, beads. Postal
service available.

Nikiski Notions

Lowther Went, South St, Cockermouth,
Cumbria CA13 9RT
t 01900 825666
Patchwork fabrics, cross-stitch, tapestry and
embroidery kits. DMC. Beads, lace and ribbon.
Russ bears.

Notions

31 Load St, Bewdley, Worcestershire
DY12 2AS
t 01299 404510
Haberdashery, tapestry & embroidery, quilting
supplies. Also curtains supplied and made.
Everything for knitting.

P E Jennison

184 Highbury Rd, Bulwell, Nottingham
NG6 9FF
t 0115 927 8376
Traditional haberdasher and draper established
1966. Stockists of wool, embroidery, zips,
buttons, leather goods and ladies' clothes.

Painters Craft-Box (t)

6 Windsor Place, Liskeard, Cornwall
PL14 4BH
t 01579 347237
e shop@craft-box.com
w www.craft-box.com
Everything for the textile artist - dyes, fibres,
threads, heat-reactive materials, Stewart Gill,
mail order and website and a café. See ad p. 30.

Peacocks Sewing & Knitting Centre

160 Station Road, Addlestone, Surrey
KT15 2BD
t 01932 846055
Tapestry wools and kits, cross-stitch kits,
embroidery silks, aida canvases, haberdashery.

Pembertons Sewing and Craft Centre (t)

21-25 Friar Street, Stirling FK8 1HA,
Scotland
t 01786 462993 **f** 01786 461998
e mail@pembertons.org
w www.pembertons.org
Everything for the sewer. Contact us for our
class list.

Petit Point

12 Montpellier Parade, Harrogate, North
Yorkshire HG1 2TJ
t 01423 565632 f 01423 503464
e needlecraft@petitpoint.co.uk
w www.petitpoint.co.uk
*Extensive range of needlepoint, cross-stitch and
embroidery designs. Needlework furniture and
accessories a speciality. Comprehensive website
for mail order. See also Shops (Stands/Furniture/
Lights).*

(The) Pincushion

1 St Marks Crescent, Maidenhead, Berkshire
SL6 5DA
t 01628 777266 f 01628 777266
e info@thepincushion.co.uk
w www.thepincushion.co.uk
*DMC, Anchor, Kreinik, Caron threads. Kits -
many different companies. Knitting yarns -
Sirdar, Patons, Wendy. Rugmaking - kits,
canvas, wools. Mail order available.*

Pins & Things

57, Bethcar St, Ebbw Vale, Gwent NP23 6HW
t 01495 350669
*We have a large selection of knitting yarns,
crochet, tapestry, cross-stitch, dress and craft
fabrics and most needlecraft accessories!*

(The) Quilted Bear

102 Whiteladies Road, Clifton, Bristol
BS8 2QY
t 0117 923 8277 f 0117 973 2771
*Cheapest for daylight lamps, quilting mats and
needlecraft accessories. Mail order available.*

Sew and So

1 Lansdown, Stroud, Glos GL5 1BB
t 01453 762895 f 01453 765289
e jackie.hall@virgin.net
*We carry an extensive range of haberdashery,
embroidery fabrics, threads, beads and cross-
stitch kits and much more. Classes available.*

Sew & So's

14 Upper Olland Street, Bungay, Suffolk
NR35 1BG
t 01986 896147 f 01379 854105
w www.sewsos.co.uk
Patchwork, quilting and embroidery supplies.

Sew On & Sew Forth

2 The Thoroughfare, Harleston, Norfolk
IP20 9AX
t 01379 853258
*Everything for your knitting and sewing needs.
We also do babywear and wedding hat hire!*

Sew-In

1 Spring Gardens, Buxton, Derbyshire
SK17 6BJ
t 01298 26636
e pauline@sew-in.co.uk
w www.sew-in.co.uk
*Dress fabrics, knit yarn, haberdashery, sewing
baskets, cross-stitch and tapestry kits.*

Sew-In of Didsbury

741 Wilmslow Road, Didsbury, Manchester
M20 6RN
t 0161 445 5861
e enquiries@knitting-and-needlework.co.uk
w www.knitting-and-needlework.co.uk
*Handknit yarns, patterns and books; cross-stitch,
tapestry and embroidery; haberdashery.*

Sew-In of Marple

46 Market St, Marple, Stockport, Cheshire
SK6 7AD
t 0161 427 2529
e enquiries@knitting-and-needlework.co.uk
w www.knitting-and-needlework.co.uk
*Handknit yarns, patterns and books; cross-stitch,
tapestry and embroidery; haberdashery.*

(The) Sewing Basket

55 Fort Street, Ayr, Ayrshire KA7 1DH
t 01292 261841
e morna@thesewingbasket.uk.com
w www.thesewingbasket.uk.com
*If you cannot find it try us - we are specialists in
threads, materials, charts, etc.*

Silver Tabby

4, Church Street, Ross-on-Wye,
Herefordshire HR9 5HN
t 01989 564950
*We stock a variety of embroidery threads, kits,
beads, etc. Also dolls house miniatures including
British-made items. Open Tuesday-Saturday.*

Spinning Jenny
The Old Smithy, Main Road, Kildwick,
Keighley, West Yorkshire BD20 9BD
t 01535 632469
*The needlework specialists - we are here to help.
Immediate mail order service.*

(The) Stitchers Patch
47 The Green, Aberdeen AB11 6NY
t 01244 585878
e avrilstitchpatch@bushinternet.com
*Fabric, threads, books, beads, tools and equipment
for patchwork and quilting, cross-stitch, tapestry,
embroidery. A huge range for all stitchers.*

(The) Stitchery
18 Deans Court, Bicester, Oxon OX26 6RD
t 01869 322966
e thestitchery@kilmory.demon.co.uk
w www.thestitchery.co.uk
*We stock a wide range of embroidery threads for
hand and machine, patchwork materials, beads,
cards, wools and craft items.*

Stitching Time
14 Haddow Street, Hamilton ML3 7HX,
Scotland
t 01698 424025 **f** 01698 424099
e getit@stitchingtime.co.uk
w www.stitchingtime.co.uk
*Embroidery and knitting stockist. Something for
everyone's needs - from the popular to the less
well known. Mail order service available.*

Storey's Upholstery
69 High St, March, Cambridgeshire PE15 9LB
t 01354 651057 **f** 01354 651057
w www.marchtown.com/adverts/storeys.htm
*DMC & Anchor specialists. Upholstery
sundries. Handknitting wool. Daylight lighting.
Rug wool. Simplicity and Burda patterns. Dylon
dyes. Fabrics. Haberdashery.*

Taylors Fabrics
Chapel Mews, North Street, Ashford, Kent
TN24 8JN
t 01233 637148
e tayfab@hotmail.com
*A huge range of curtain, dress and craft fabrics,
net curtains, haberdashery, ribbons. Everything
for the home sewer and more!*

Thomason of Clitheroe
19 Moor Lane, Clitheroe, Lancashire
BB7 1BE
t 01200 426228
*Everything for the needlewoman. Sewing
machine sales and repairs. Kits, fabrics,
haberdashery and crafts.*

Thomason Sewing Centre
25 Briercliffe Road, Burnley, Lancashire
BB10 1XH
t 01282 432983
*Everything for the needlewoman. Sewing
machine sales and repairs. Kits, fabrics,
haberdashery and crafts.*

Thread-Bear
33 Killigrew Street, Falmouth, Cornwall
TR11 3PW
t 01326 319358
e threadbear@compuserve.com
*Haberdashery shop with Daylight lamps, sewing
machines, fabrics (we specialise in quilting), soft
toy components, needlework kits.*

White Rose Sewing Machine Company
17 Sagar Street, Castleford, W Yorks
WF10 1AG
t 01977 553198 **f** 01977 553198
*Major stockist of Janome sewing machines.
Stockists of Horn cabinets, DMC threads and
many other craft products. In-house tuition
provided.*

Windmill Crafts
33 High St, Gravesend, Kent DA11 0AZ
t 01474 329777
w www.windmill-crafts.co.uk
*Suppliers of DMC, Anchor, Appletons, cotton
fabrics, dolls' houses, beads, rubber stamps,
cross-stitch and tapestry kits, rugmaking, dyes.*

(The) Winky Birds
2c Grosvenor Road, Urmston, Manchester
M41 5AQ
t 0161 755 3629 **f** 0161 755 3629
e TheWinkyBirds@aol.com
w thewinkybirds.co.uk
*Situated near the Trafford Centre, an art and
crafts shop offering needlework, threads, beads,
workshops and a friendly welcome.*

Witney Knitting Centre
61 High St, Witney, Oxfordshire OX28 6JA
t 01993 702772
Wide range of knitting yarns, dress fabrics, needlework products and haberdashery. Also at 57 Parsons Street, Banbury (Banbury Sewing Centre).

(The) Wool & Fabric Shop
Town Hall Buildings, Market Place, Brigg, North Lincolnshire DN20 8ER
t 01652 653136
The specialists for knitting yarns, tapestry and needlecraft kits and extensive haberdashery. Fashion, furnishing, craft fabrics in remnants or rolls.

Wye Needlecraft
2 Royal Oak Place, Matlock St, Bakewell, Derbyshire DE45 1HD
t 01629 815198 **f** 01629 814100
e wye@globalnet.co.uk
w www.wye.co.uk
A winning needlecraft shop, offering both service and a great selection. Well worth a visit. You will not be disappointed.

Kit Specialists

Border Crafts
9 Castlegate, Berwick-upon-Tweed, Northumberland TD15 1JS
t 01289 305349 **f** 01289 305349
e mccreeth@yahoo.com
Designer knitwear, découpage pictures, cross-stitch kits, glass painting supplies, prints and framing, etc.

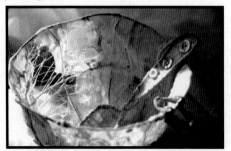

Detail of 'Time for Tea', Priscilla Jones, see Textile Artists and Designers, p. 100.

Susan Lethbridge Designs
Devonia House, Fore St, Milverton, Taunton, Somerset TA4 1JU
t 01823 401373 **f** 01823 401362
e susan@susan-lethbridge-designs.co.uk
w www.susan-lethbridge-designs.co.uk
Tapestry kits for all ages and abilities, clearly printed canvases and wools packaged and presented to enthuse the hesitant!

Knitting/Crochet

A & B Woolshop
2 White Hart Mews, Southgate, Sleaford, Lincolnshire NG34 7RY
t 01529 413143
Stockists of top brand yarns, crafts, cross-stitch kits, tapestry kits and a full range of haberdashery.

A Stitch in Time
197 Cowbridge Road East, Canton, Cardiff CF11 9AJ
t 029 2022 6828
Haberdashery, knitting wools, cross stitch, embroidery.

A Twaddle
56 Main Street, Ballymoney, County Antrim BT53 6AL
t 028 2766 4159
Stockists of children's and adults' handknit Arans and fashion knits. Large stock of tapestries and cross stitch.

Ann-Louise   **t**
204 Copnor Road, Portsmouth, Hampshire PO3 5DA
t 023 9264 4242
For quality wool, knitting patterns, cross-stitch, DMC threads and associated items. Open 6 days a week 8.30-5.30.

Banff Knitting Centre   **t**
10a Boyndie Street, Banff, Aberdeenshire AB45 1DY
t 01261 815857 **f** 01261 815857
Sirdar hand knitting yarns, machine knitting yarns, knitting machines, accessories.

Bobbins

Wesley Hall, Church Street, Whitby, North Yorkshire YO22 4DE
t 01947 600585 **f** 01947 600585
e bobbins@global.net.co.uk
w www.bobbins.co.uk
Specialist in 5-ply fishermen's sweater kits and denim cotton knitting kits. Rowan stockist, Colinette hand-painted yarns.

Brenda's

104a, Peabody Rd, Farnborough, Hampshire GU14 6DY
t 01252 541923
e brendasschoolwear@hotmail.com
w www.brendasschoolwear.com
Brenda's stocks a good range of Sirdar, Wendy, Patons yarns, knitting patterns and haberdashery.

Budget Wools

Clarence Parade, Cheltenham, Glos GL50 3PA
t 01242 522473
Your specialist wool shop in Gloucestershire. Stockists of Sirdar, Patons, Wendy, Jaeger and many more!

D & M Tones

7 Market Place, Guisborough, Cleveland TS14 6BN
t 01287 632348
We are stockists for Jaeger Wools, Sirdar, Paton & Baldwin, Stylecraft. Tapestries, Twilleys tapestry wools, tapestry canvases and embroidered goods.

Dee Yarns

44 Church Street, Flint, Clwyd CH6 5AE
t 01352 731575
We offer an extensive range of knitting yarns including Sirdar and Wendy. Also needlework kits plus an outstanding collection of childrenswear.

Ennis Hobby's

26-28, Alexandra Road, Clevedon, Avon BS21 7QH
t 01275 794410 **f** 01275 794410
e sales@ennishobbys.co.uk
w www.ennishobbys.co.uk
A family-run business with lots of wool, DMC silks full range, crochet cottons and haberdashery items, patchwork & quilting.

Eve Maxwell

8 The Parade, Cherry Willingham, Lincoln LN3 4JL
t 01522 751232
Main stockists of Sirdar and Stylecraft. Ribbons, cottons, embroidery silks and general haberdashery.

Forfar Knitting Centre

103 East High St, Forfar, Angus DD8 2EQ
t 01307 468151
Hand and machine knitting. Sewing machine sales and repairs.

HMK Wools

47 Flixton Road, Urmston, Manchester M41 5AN
t 0161 748 5971
e norman@accsysmail.com
Family business established 1937 retailing hand-knitting yarns. Also school uniform stockist and agent for Cash's personalised embroidered name tapes.

Hooked on Crochet

60 Market St, Ulverston, Cumbria LA12 7LT
t 01229 588558 **f** 01539 530617
A crochet wonderland. Over 500 patterns, hooks, yarns and tuition. Commissions undertaken.

Janes of Fishguard

14 High St, Fishguard, Pembrokeshire SA65 9AR
t 01348 874443
Knitting and crochet. Also haberdashery, kits, threads, buttons, fabric dyes, ribbons, braids, lace.

Kangaroo

70 High St, Lewes, East Sussex BN7 1XG
t 01273 478554 **f** 01273 483909
e sue@kangaroo.uk.com
w www.kangaroo.uk.com
Wide range of knitting yarns, patterns and accessories.

Knitcraft

25 Fore Street, Pool, Redruth, Cornwall TR15 3DZ
t 01209 216661
Wools and patterns for hand knitters. Stylecraft, Wendy stockists. Bramwell combs for machine knitters. Haberdashery. Mail order available.

La Tienda
7 Trysull Rd, Bradmore, Wolverhampton,
West Midlands WV3 7HX
t 01902 336644
*Wool shop with some cross stitch. Stockists of
Sirdar, Patons, Jaeger, Wendy, Robin &
Stylecraft. Big range of buttons and haberdashery.*

Maple St Stores
2 Maple St, Lincoln, Lincolnshire LN5 8QT
t 01522 531979
*General store that also offers knitting wool. Some
Studley, some King Cole, some Woolcraft.*

MSR Woolcraft
39 Castle Street, Forfar, Angus DD8 3AE
t 01307 463764
*Large selection of Sirdar and Wendy wools.
Hand knitting specialists.*

Nen's Den
2 Fridays Court, High Street, Ringwood,
Hampshire BH24 1AB
t 01425 480426
*Stockists of Sirdar, Wendy, Peter Pan and
Stylecraft wools. Also cross-stitch, tapestry,
embroidery silks and haberdashery.*

(The) New Wool Shop
High St, Bishops Waltham, Southampton,
Hampshire SO32 1AB
t 01489 891169
*Typical old-fashioned wool shop - tiny but with
elasticated sides! Stockists of Sirdar and
Hayfield. Haberdashery.*

Olveston House
22 Westward Road, Cainscross, Stroud,
Gloucestershire GL5 4JQ
t 01453 764887
Sirdar/Stylecraft wool stockist.

Prescot Knitting Co Ltd 🅣
32 Eccleston St, Prescot, Merseyside L34 5QJ
t 0151 426 5264
w www.prescotknitting.co.uk
*For all the leading brands of hand knitting yarns
and needlecraft including Sirdar, Wendy, Jaeger,
Rowan, DMC, Anchor, Heritage, etc.*

R D Bishop & Sons Ltd
Pioneer Market, Winston Way, Ilford, Essex
IG1 2RD
t 020 8478 0515
*A very large wool retailer. Stockists of 1000s of
knitting leaflets and all major wool manufacturers.*

R G & B Lloyd
13 West Street, Crewe, Cheshire CW1 3HD
t 01270 212559 **f** 01270 212559
*Extensive range of yarns from 2-ply to super
chunky. Craftime dolls and haberdashery -
established over 40 years.*

Rendells
28a Abbeygate Street, Bury St Edmunds,
Suffolk IP33 1UN
t 01284 764196
*Wool shop established over 40 years.
Comprehensive range of wools.*

Sally Carr Designs 🅣
The Yarn Shop, 31 High Street, Totnes,
Devon TQ9 5NP
t 01803 863060 **f** 01803 863060
*Stockists of Colinette, Rowan, Sirdar, King Cole,
etc. Accessories and hand-dyed buttons. Help
always given where possible.*

(The) Shetland Connection
491 Lawnmarket, Edinburgh EH1 2NT
t 0131 225 3525
*Main stockist Shetland wool and knitted goods.
Mail order available.*

Sky
11 Albion St, Rugeley, Staffordshire WS15 2BY
t 01889 576551 **f** 01889 576551
*Knitting/crochet/tapestry/embroidery/framing
service.*

Superwools
9 Tiviot Dale, Stockport, Cheshire SK1 1TA
t 0161 477 5501
*Stockist of Sirdar and Wendy hand knitting
yarns, knitting patterns and books.*

Wells Knitting Centre
5 Mill Street, Wells, Somerset BA5 2AS
t 01749 677548
*Large stocks of yarns for hand, machine knitting
and crochet. 1000s of patterns. Haberdashery,
rug kits. Garments knitted to order.*

(The) Wool Shed
Alford Heritage Centre, Mart Road, Alford,
Aberdeenshire AB33 8BZ
t 01975 562906
*Rowan and Colinette yarns suitable for
handknitting, weaving and embroidery. Spinning
and weaving equipment and knitwear. Spinning/
knitting tuition available.*

(The) Wool Shop
3 Market Buildings, High Street, Scunthorpe,
South Humberside DN15 6SY
t 01724 852074
e vaughan@cwcom.net
w www.thewoolshop.cwc.net
*Supplying quality knitting and crochet yarns
and patterns plus a large range of needlecraft
kits. Try our website.*

Wool-Mart
51 Cambridge Rd, Kingston upon Thames,
Surrey KT1 3NS
t 020 8549 1944
*Price-wise knitting wools! Small amount of
haberdashery.*

Patchwork and Quilting

(The) Bramble Patch
West Street, Weedon, Northants NN7 4QU
t 01327 342212 **f** 01327 342212
e bramblepatch@qualityservice.com
w www.thebramblepatch.co.uk
*Specialist patchwork and quilting shop with huge
range of fabrics and offering numerous workshops held in spacious, well-equipped workroom.*

Country Threads
2 Pierrepont Place, Bath BA1 1JX
t 01225 480056 **f** 01225 480056
*Patchwork and quilting supplies. 1500 bolts of
100% cotton fabrics, books, tools and comprehensive workshop programme.*

Green Mountain Quilts & Crafts
4a Penton Avenue, Staines, Middx TW18 2NB
t 01784 452077
e m.p.j.doyle@talk21.com
*Seven hundred bolts of fabric - classes for all
levels of quilters - friendly knowledgable staff -
patterns and kits - close to Heathrow.*

House of Patchwork
Units 18/19 Tower Centre, Hoddesdon,
Herts EN11 8UB
t 01992 447544 **f** 01992 446892
e lesley@houseofpatchwork.co.uk
w www.houseofpatchwork.co.uk
*Specialist patchwork/quilting shop providing
wide variety of classes for all levels of students.
Expert and helpful advice. Friendly atmosphere.*

Inca Studio
10 Duke Street, Princes Risborough, Bucks
HP27 0AT
t 01844 343343 **f** 01844 201263
e studioinca@aol.com
w www.incastudio.com
*The patchwork store in the Chilterns. 1500+
100% cotton fabrics. Hand and machine threads,
wadding, notions and books galore.*

Joseph's Coat
The Limes, Cowbridge CF71 7BJ, Wales
t 01446 775620
e josephscoat@tesco.net
*Tremendous choice of fabrics. Workshops and
classes for small and large groups. Expert and
friendly advice on all patchwork projects.*

Moor Silks & Quilts
8 Market Street, Tavistock, Devon PL19 0DA
t 01822 612624 **f** 01822 611106
e info@moor-silks-and-quilts.co.uk
w www.moor-silks and-quilts.co.uk
*Leading southwest needlecraft centre, supplying
quilting, embroidery, Bernina sewing machines
and workshops.*

Patchwork Corner
51 Belswains Lane, Hemel Hempstead,
Herts HP3 9PW
t 01442 259000 **f** 01442 259000
e patchworkcorner@fsmail.net
*We stock everything for your patchwork and
quilting supplies. Workshops and courses run
throughout the year, beginners and intermediate.*

Patchwork Plus ⓣ
129 Station Rd, Cark in Cartmel,
Grange-over-Sands, Cumbria LA11 7NY
t 01539 559009 f 01539 559009
e sales@patchworkplus.co.uk
w www.patchworkplus.co.uk
*A wide range of patchwork and quilting supplies
plus needlecraft books, tapestries, cross-stitch and
embroidery in beautiful south Lakeland.*

Patchworks ⓣ
1-3 Millar Crescent, Edinburgh EH10 5HN
t 0131 477 3555 f 0131 477 3558
e patchworks01@hotmail.com
w www.patchworks-edinburgh.com
*Over 1500 bolts of fabric, books, haberdashery
and workshops held on the premises.
Group visits welcome*

Piecemakers ⓣ
13 Manor Green Road, Epsom, Surrey
KT19 8RA
t 01372 743161
w www.piecemakers.co.uk
*At Piecemakers you will find an exciting range
of fabrics to suit your patchwork needs. Classes
for all levels.*

Quilters Haven ⓣ
68 High Street, Wickham Market, Suffolk
IP13 0QU
t 01728 746275 f 01394 610525
e quilters.haven@btinternet.com
w www.quilters-haven.co.uk
*Quilt shop with teaching rooms and gallery.
Mail order - 1000s of fabrics. Over 500 books,
including own publications.*

(The) Quilting Bee ⓣ
14, Enfield Rd, Enfield, Middlesex EN2 7HW
t 020 8364 5237
*All quilting supplies, books, kits, patterns. 1500
cotton fabrics for all crafts, workshops, group
visits welcomed. Beginners' classes.*

Serendipity
6a Station Road, Bovey Tracey, Devon
TQ13 9AL
t 01626 836246 f 01626 836768
e serendipitycrafts@yahoo.com
*Not just another fabric shop! Seredipity uniquely
also exhibits and sells quilts made mainly by
quilters of the southwest.*

Sew Creative ⓣ
Wroxham Barns, Tunstead Road, Hoveton,
Norfolk NR12 8QU
t 01603 781665
e sewcreative@sylvia79.fsbusiness.co.uk
*Workshops in patchwork, quilting, embroidery,
beading, national and international tutors. Over
1800 bolts of fabric plus all notions.*

Sunflower Fabrics ⓣ
157-159 Castle Road, Bedford MK40 3RS
t 01234 273819
e maggie@SunflowerFabrics.com
w www.SunflowerFabrics.com
*Specialist patchwork and quilting supplier -
fabric, books and other equipment. Our own
patterns and an excellent website.*

Village Fabrics ⓣ
4-5 St Leonard's Square, Wallingford,
Oxfordshire OX10 0AS
t 01491 204100 f 01491 204013
e info@villagefabrics.co.uk
w www.villagefabrics.co.uk
*Patchwork and quilting fabric (100% cotton
from America), books, notions, haberdashery,
patterns, Husqvarna Studio, furnishing fabrics.
Mail order. Classes.*

White Cottage Country Crafts ⓣ
24 Post Office Road, Seisdon,
Wolverhampton, West Midlands WV5 7HA
t 01902 896917
e Jacqueline.Taylor@ ukgateway.net
*A wide selection of patchwork and quilting books,
fabrics and supplies. Day classes and weekend
residential classes available.*

Woodbine Country Crafts ⓣ
Market Place, Hope, Hope Valley,
Derbyshire S33 6RH
t 01433 621821 f 01433 621821
e judith@woodbinecafe.freeserve.co.uk
w www.woodbinecafe.freeserve.co.uk
*Specialist patchwork & quilting shop. 1500 bolts,
wide range for all tastes. Friendly, helpful staff.*

Sewing Machine Sales

Ashford Sewing Centre
6 New Rents, Ashford, Kent TN23 1JH
t 01233 620948
Full range of new and second-hand sewing machines. Sales and full service on all makes. Haberdashery, wools, crafts.

Binder's
67 Fengate, Peterborough, Cambridgeshire PE1 5BA
t 01733 340449
Sewing machine sales, spares, repairs plus haberdashery.

Bredons of Taunton
3 Eastgate, East St, Taunton, Somerset TA1 3NB
t 01823 272450 **f** 01823 272450
e info@bredons.co.uk
w www.bredons.co.uk
Massive choice of new and reconditioned sewing machines at unbeatable prices. Overlockers, cabinets, iron presses, fabrics, tuition and mail order.

Brewers Sewing Machines
458 Dudley Road, Wolverhampton, West Midlands WV2 3AF
t 01902 458885 **f** 01902 458885
w www.brewerssewing.co.uk
Industrial/domestic. Sales/service. Local authority/educational suppliers. Presses/cabinets. Bernina. Brother. Janome. Singer. Elna. Overlockers, flatbeds, blindhemmers, upholstery machines.

Direct Sewing Machine Supply Co
46 Sandy Park Road, Brislington, Bristol, Avon BS4 3PF
t 0117 977 8216 **f** 0117 977 8216
e info@directsewingmachinesupplies.co.uk
w www.directsewing.co.uk
Established for forty years. Same owner. All makes of machine supplied.

Elgin Sewing Centre
19a, Batchen St, Elgin, Morayshire IV30 1BH
t 01343 549191 **f** 01343 549191
e sales@elginsewcentre.co.uk
w www.elginsewcentre.co.uk
Secure online shop for all makes of sewing machines, accessories, etc.

Exeter Sewing Machine Co
7 Heavitree Road, Exeter, Devon EX1 2LD
t 01392 275660 **f** 01392 275661
e exesew@eclipse.co.uk
w www.exetersewing.co.uk
Sewing machines, most brands, patchwork and quilting supplies, dress and craft fabrics, millinery supplies, good range of classes.

Fergusons Sewing Machines
19 The Market, Scotch St, Carlisle, Cumbria CA3 8QX
t 01228 537612
Sales and service of all makes of domestic sewing machines.

Fox Sewing Machines
60 Babington Lane, Derby, Derbyshire DE1 1SX
t 01332 347941
Specialists in Bernina and Janome. Brilliant, old-fashioned shop service. Fabrics, embroidery threads, notions. Very friendly shop - give us a visit!

Hobkirks Sewing Centres
24 Bolton Street, Bury, Lancashire BL90LQ
t 0161 764 4450 **f** 0161 764 4450
e info@hobkirk.co.uk
w www.hobkirk.co.uk
Husqvarna studio, Janome, Toyota, full range of machines and accessories. Haberdashery, patterns, needlecraft, dressforms, horn cabinets, daylight lamps and magnifiers.

Homecraft (Blackpool)
62 Abingdon St, Blackpool, Lancashire FY1 1NH
t 01253 626729
Sewing machine sales and accessories. Sewing machine repairs. Sew be crafty and make your way to Homecraft.

Husqvarna Studio Nottingham
90 Lower Parliament St, Nottingham NG1 1EH
t 0115 988 1550 **f** 0115 988 1552
e info@husqvarnastudio.co.uk
w www.husqvarnastudio.co.uk
Specialists of Husqvarna Viking sewing and overlocking machines. Tuition and courses in many subjects. Fabrics, haberdashery and all your sewing needs.

Husqvarna Viking Studio 🌐
4 Savoy Buildings, 27 Truro Rd, St Austell,
Cornwall PL25 5JE
t 01726 72506
e sewing.staustell@lineone.net
*Full range of Husqvarna Viking sewing
machines. All models of sewing machines
serviced and repaired. Creative sewing
workshops and tuition.*

Kettering Sewing Centre 🌐
1-9 Overstone Rd, Northampton NN1 3JL
t 01604 637200 **f** 01604 637200
e info@sewing-centres.co.uk
w sewing-centres.co.uk
*Domestic sewing machine and overlock
specialists, expert service and repairs. Design
software training and demonstrations.*

Lewisham & Deptford Sewing Machine Co
181, Deptford High St, London SE8 3NT
t 020 8692 1077 **f** 020 8692 0228
e deptford@sewingmachines.fsnet.co.uk
w www.sewingmachinesuk.co.uk
*Repair specialists, suppliers of new and used,
industrial and domestic sewing machiines and
overlockers. Agents for all leading makes.*

MacCulloch & Wallis
25 Dering Street, London W1
t 020 7629 0311 **f** 020 7491 2481
e macculloch@psilink.co.uk
w www.macculloch-wallis.co.uk
*Bernina & Janome stockists, sales and service,
part exchange, free demonstration, no obligation.
Suppliers of fine fabrics and haberdashery
since 1902.*

(The) Pincushion 🌐
5 Ashby Square, Loughborough,
Leicestershire LE11 5AA
t 01509 210747
*New/used sewing machines, repairs and spares to
most makes. 30 years' experience. Sewing
threads/patterns/needles/haberdashery.*

Reads of Winchester
1 St Thomas St, Winchester, Hampshire
SO23 9HE
t 01962 850950
*Sewing machine sales and repairs. Some haber-
dashery. Demonstrations on all machines given.*

Rona Sewing Machines 🌐
120 High St, Waltham Cross, Herts EN8 7BX
t 01992 719739 **f** 01992 653375
e sales@ronasewingmachines.co.uk
w ronasewingmachines.co.uk
*Sales and repairs of sewing machines, overlockers
and industrial machines. Sewing classes and
tuition. Plus fabrics, wool and haberdashery.*

Scunthorpe Sewing Machine Centre
115 Mary St, Scunthorpe, North Lincs DN15 6LA
t 01724 849909
e derek@stamper.freeserve.co.uk
*Established 25 years with a friendly service
and competitive prices in both domestic and
industrial sewing machines.*

Sewing Centre Bridlington
1, Queen St, Bridlington, North Humberside
YO15 2SF
t 01262 603057 **f** 01262 603057
*Sewing machine sales, repairs and servicing.
Stocking fabric and haberdashery.*

(The) Sewing Knitting & Handicraft Centre
125 Mostyn St, Llandudno, Gwynedd LL30 2PE
t 01492 875269
e enquiries@sewingmachinesdirect.co.uk
w www.sewingmachinesdirect.co.uk
*Stockists and main dealers for most leading makes.
Suppliers and service agents to local authorities.
Large range of reconditioned machines.*

Sewing Machine Centre
23a Bury St, Stowmarket, Suffolk IP14 1HA
t 01449 676424
*Sewing machine repairs and service to most
makes and ages. New and used machine sales,
parts and haberdashery.*

Sewing Machine Exchange
21 Charles St, Wrexham, Clwyd LL13 8BT
t 01978 266746
*Suppliers of quality sewing machines, overlockers, cabi-
nets and iron presses. Janome, Elna, Horn, Frister, etc.*

TDA Sewing
11a Irvine St, Leigh, Lancashire WN7 1ND
t 01942 261942
e tda@sewingmachinerepairs.uk.com
w sewingmachinerepairs.uk.com
Sewing machine service and repair/sales.

Soft Furnishing

City Fabrics (Cardiff) Ltd
107, Tewkesbury Road, Cheltenham,
Gloucestershire GL51 9DW
t 01242 541212 **f** 01242 541213
e info@city-fabrics.com
w www.city-fabrics.com
The new soft furnishers of Cheltenham, offering a wide range of innovative fabrics with a first-class made-to-measure service.

(The) Curtain Works
23, Main Street, Barton under Needwood,
Burton-on-Trent, Staffordshire DE13 8AA
t 01283 716754 **f** 01283 716754
Soft furnishing and curtain fabrics by order. Handmade curtains.

Redwood Fabrics
Unit 2, Meadow Lane Trading Est, Meadow
Lane, Nottingham NG2 3HD
t 0115 985 2255
e amanda@redwood.joy-inter.net
w www.redwood-fabrics.com
Import and export fabric merchants. Fashion and furnishing fabrics. Wholesale and retail. Commission agents also. See also Shops (Fabrics).

Stands/Furniture/Lights

Petit Point
12 Montpellier Parade, Harrogate, North
Yorkshire HG1 2TJ
t 01423 565632 **f** 01423 503464
e needlecraft@petitpoint.co.uk
w www.petitpoint.co.uk
Extensive range of needlepoint, cross stitch and embroidery designs. Needlework furniture and accessories a speciality. Comprehensive website for mail order. See also Shops (General Needlecraft).

Weaving/Spinning/Feltmaking

Raw Fibres
Old Signalbox, Station Workshops, Robin
Hood's Bay, North Yorks YO22 4RA
t 01947 880632 **f** 01947 881119
e rosemary@beaconhillfarm.fsnet.co.uk
w www.brigantia.co.uk
Handspun/hand-dyed fibres/yarns for creative feltmaking, embroidery, spinning, weaving. Shetland fleeces, agents for spinning/weaving equipment. Open by arrangement.

Shops by area

Abbreviations

Art = Art Materials
Dyes = Dyes/Silk Paints
Emb = Embroidery
Gen = General Needlecraft
Knit = Knitting/Crochet
P&Q = Patchwork & Quilting
Fab = Fabrics
Sew = Sewing Machine Sales
Soft Furn = Soft Furnishing
Stands = Stands/ Furniture/Lights
Weave = Weaving/ Spinning/Feltmaking

East Anglia

A & B Woolshop (Knit)
Bears & Stitches (Gen)
Binder's (Sew)
Branch Drapers House (Gen)
Buttons And Bows (Gen)
Cooper & Baumber (Gen)
(The) Crafty Patch (Gen)
Don't Tell Mother (Gen)
Eve Maxwell (Knit)
(The) Fabric Company (Fab)
Fabric Warehouse (Fab)
Fantastic Fibres (Gen)
Hemsleys (Gen)
Knickerbean Ltd (Fab)
Louanne Fabrics (Fab)
Maple St Stores (Knit)
Quilters Haven (P&Q)
Rendells (Knit)
Sew Creative (P&Q)
Sew & So's (Gen)
Sew On & Sew Forth (Gen)
Sewing Machine Centre (Sew)
Storey's Upholstery (Gen)
Sunflower Fabrics (P&Q)

Midlands

(The) Bramble Patch (P&Q)
Brewers Sewing Machines (Sew)
Burford Needlecraft (Gen)
Camelot Crafts (Gen)
City Fabrics (Cardiff) Ltd (Soft Furn)
Cloth Market of Stamford (Fab)
Country Fabrics (Gen)
Crafts 'n' Sew On (Gen)
(The) Curtain Works (Soft Furn)
Ebonique Designs (Fab)
(The) Embroidery Shop (Gen)
Esberger Fabrics (Fab)
Fabric Barn (Gen)
Forge Mill Needle Musuem (Gen)
Fourmark Art & Craft Centre (Gen)
Fox Sewing Machines (Sew)
(The) Frame Workshop (Frames)
Greyhouse Fabrics (Fab)
House of Sandersons (Fab)
Husqvarna Studio Nottingham (Sew)
Jai Sareetex (Fab)
Kettering Sewing Centre (Sew)
Kisko Fabrics (Fab)
La Tienda (Knit)
Laurel Crafts (Gen)
(The) Needleworker (Gen)
Notions (Gen)
P E Jennison (Sew)
(The) Pincushion (Sew)
Redwood Fabrics (Fab; Soft Furn)
Sew-In (Gen)
Silver Tabby (Gen)
Sky (Knit)
Tahim Drapers (Fab)
Textile Traders (Fab)
(The) Stitchery (Gen)
White Cottage Country Crafts (P&Q)
Wye Needlecraft (Gen)

North Central

(The) Skep (Fab)
Woodbine Country Crafts (P&Q)

North East

A M S Fabrics (Fab)
Artefacts of Whitby (Gen)
Bobbins (Knit)
Border Crafts (Kits)
Craftmill (Gen)
Cross Stitch Corner (Gen)
D & M Tones (Knit)
Esberger Fabrics (Fab)
Jenny Scott's Creative Embroidery (Emb)
Kay Krafts (Gen)

85

North East cont.

Marion's Needlecraft & Miniatures (Gen)
Meynells Ltd (Gen)
Petit Point (Gen; Stands)
Raw Fibres (Weave)
Scunthorpe Sewing Machine Centre (Sew)
Sewing Centre Bridlington (Sew)
(The) Wool & Fabric Shop (Gen)
(The) Wool Shop (Knit)
White Rose Sewing Machine Company (Gen)

North West

ArtiSan's (Art; Dyes)
Arts & Crafts Studio (Gen)
Auntie Pat's Place (Gen)
(The) Bankrupt Shop Ltd (Fab)
(The) Curtain House (Fab)
Fabric Warehouse (Fab)
Fergusons Sewing Machines (Sew)
HMK Wools (Knit)
Hobby's (Gen)
Hobkirks Sewing Centres (Gen)
Hobkirks Sewing Centres (Sew)
Homecraft (Blackpool) (Sew)
Hooked on Crochet (Knit)
Jenkins Sewing Centre (Fab)
Joan Weir Fabrics (Fab)
June Fabrics (Fab)
Just Sew (Gen)
Knickers n' Lace (Gen)
Knitting & Sewing Centre (Gen)
McNeely Discount Soft Furnishings (Fab)
Mears Ghyll Fabrics (Fab)
Nikiski Notions (Gen)
Patchwork Plus (P&Q)
Prescot Knitting Co Ltd (Knit)
R G & B Lloyd (Knit)
Sew-In of Didsbury (Gen)
Sew-In of Marple (Gen)
(The) Sewing Box (Fab)
Spinning Jenny (Gen)
Superwools (Knit)
T D A Sewing (Sew)
Thomason of Clitheroe (Gen)
Thomason Sewing Centre (Gen)
Variegations (Emb)
(The) Winky Birds (Gen)

Northern Ireland

A Twaddle (Knit)

Scotland

Banff Knitting Centre (Knit)
Canny Crafts (Gen)
Dorrie Doodle (Art)
Elgin Sewing Centre (Sew)
Forfar Knitting Centre (Knit)
Just Sew Fabrics (Fab)
Little Stitches (Gen)
MSR Woolcraft (Knit)

Nifty Needles (Gen)
Patchworks (P&Q)
Pats (Fab)
Pembertons Sewing and Craft Centre (Gen)
(The) Sewing Basket (Gen)
(The) Shetland Connection (Knit)
(The) Stitchers Patch (Gen)
Stitching Time (Gen)
(The) Wool Shed (Knit)

South Central

Brenda's (Knit)
Country Crafts (Gen)
Crown Needlework (Emb)
Knickerbean Ltd (Fab)
Knitters Corner (Gen)
(The) New Wool Shop (Knit)
Reads of Winchester (Sew)
Sew Elegant (Fab)

South East

Alison's (Gen)
Ann-Louise (Knit)
Anne & Paul's Feltham Woolshop (Gen)
Art Van Go (Art; Dyes)
Ashford Sewing Centre (Sew)
Blanshard Fabrics (Fab)
Broadwick Silks Ltd (Fab)
CRA (Art)
C & H Fabrics Ltd (Fab)
Choice (Gen)
(The) Cloth Store (Fab)
Essex Fabric Warehouse (Fab)
Green Mountain Quilts & Crafts (P&Q)
Hadson Exclusive Fabrics (Fab)
Hangzhou Silks (Fab)
Hansson Silks (Fab)
House of Patchwork (P&Q)
Inca Studio (P&Q)
J E M's Sewing and Needlework Centre (Gen)
Just Sew (Gen)
Kangaroo (Knit)
Knickerbean Ltd (Fab)
Lady Sew & Sew (Gen)
Lewisham & Deptford Sewing Machine Co (Sew)
Lili Fabrics (Fab)
MacCulloch & Wallis (Sew)
Michael's Bridal Fabrics (Fab)
Needle & Thread (Gen)
Nen's Den (Knit)
Newnham Court Crafts (Gen)
Patchwork Corner (P&Q)
Peacocks Sewing & Knitting Centre (Gen)
Piecemakers (P&Q)
(The) Pincushion (Gen)
(The) Quilting Bee (P&Q)
R D Bishop & Sons Ltd (Knit)
R H Sands & Sons (Fab)
Rainbow Silks (Dyes)

Rona Sew (Sew)
Saffron (Fab)
Sew Fantastic (Fab)
Taylors Fabrics (Gen)
Village Fabrics (P&Q)
Warris Vianni & Co (Fab)
Windmill Crafts (Gen)
Witney Knitting Centre (Gen)
Wool-Mart (Knit)

South West

(The) Ball of Wool (Gen)
Bredons of Taunton (Sew)
Budget Wools (Knit)
Ceres Crafts (Art)
(The) Cloth Shop (Fab)
(The) Cotton Mills (Fab)
Country Threads (P&Q)
(The) Craft Centre (Gen)
Crazy Cross Stitcher (Gen)
Creative Crafts (Gen)
curtainfabricsLtd.co.uk (Fab)
Direct Sewing Machine Supply Co (Sew)
Ennis Hobby's (Knit)
Evangelines (Gen)
Exeter Sewing Machine Co (Sew)
Fabric Magic (Fab)
From Debbie Cripps (Emb)
Hellerslea Fabrics (Fab)
Husqvarna Viking Studio (Sew)
K Fabrics (Gen)
Knickerbean Ltd (Fab)
Knitcraft (Knit)
Moor Silks & Quilts (P&Q)
Olveston House (Knit)
Painters Craft-Box (Gen)
(The) Quilted Bear (Gen)
Sally Carr Designs (Knit)
Serendipity (P&Q)
Sew and So (Gen)
Susan Lethbridge Designs (Kits)
Thread-Bear (Gen)
Wells Knitting Centre (Knit)

Wales

A Stitch in Time (Knit)
Dee Yarns (Knit)
Hotch Potch (Fab)
In-Fabrics (Fab)
Janes of Fishguard (Knit)
Joseph's Coat (P&Q)
Maesteg Knitting Crafts (Gen)
Marion's Patchworks (Gen)
Pins & Things (Gen)
(The) Sewing Knitting & Handicraft Centre (Sew)
Sewing Machine Exchange (Sew)

Specialist Breaks and Holidays

Ardess Craft Centre
Kesh, Co Fermanagh, BT93 1NX, N. Ireland
t 02868 631267 **f** 02868 631267
e ardess@lineone.net
w www.fermanaghcraft.com/ardesscraft
*Dorothy Pendry teaches spinning, weaving,
natural dyeing; fleece from her Jacob sheep. Also
lace, embroidery courses.*

Artisan
Laceby Manor, Laceby, Lincs DN37 7EA
t 01472 872217
e artisan.retreats@lineone.net
*Day classes and residential stitching retreats in a
beautiful Georgian manor house. Wide choice of
topics for all ability levels.*

Pie Chambers - Textiles
16 Catherine Hill, Frome, Somerset BA11 1B2
t 01373 455690 **f** 01373 455992
e pie@tulsi.freeserve.co.uk
*Coach House Blues. Exciting textile courses:
kilim weaving, resist dyeing and quilting - all
with a hint of indigo!*

Creative Days, The Old Vicarage
The Old Vicarage, Llansilin, Oswestry,
Shropshire SY10 7PX
t 01691 791345 **f** 01691 791345
e pam@creativedays.co.uk
w www.creativedays.co.uk
*Courses in arts, textiles, crafts and country
skills. One-day and residential in rural
Shropshire. Free full programme on request.*

Creative Stitches
34 La Grande Piece, St Peter, Jersey JE3 7AE
t 01534 482097 **f** 01534 482097
e creativestitches@yahoo.com
w www.creativestitches.co.uk
*Cross stitch and mixed craft courses in Jersey.
Suitable for all abilities and ideal for those
holidaying alone.*

Fabric & Threads Plus
3 Grand Rue, Laz, 29520, Brittany, France
t +33 2 98 26 87 23
e thomson.g@voila.fr
*Textile holiday courses with Gill Thompson in
Brittany, France. Patchwork, quilting, embroidery
and much more. Pick-up services. Outings inclusive.*

Pat Gibson
The Studio, Swn-y-Gwynt, Caersws, Powys
SY17 5HH
t 01686 689048
e pat.gibson@tesco.net
w www.intatexnet.co.uk/lacedesign
*2-, 3- and 5-day courses in needlelace, machine
embroidery and much more, in mid-Wales. Full
programme on request. See also Textile Artists
and Designers.*

Great Breaks - Acorn Activities
PO Box 120, Hereford HR4 8YB
t 08707 405055 **f** 08707 405066
e info@great-breaks.org
w www.great-breaks.org
*Great Breaks organises activity and special
interest breaks for all ages.*

Great Divide Weaving School
PO Box 100, Divide, Colorado 80814, USA
t +1 719 687 3249
e info@greatdivideweavingschool.com
w www.greatdivideweavingschool.com
*One-week and two-week tapestry workshops.
Twelve tapestry techniques first week. Pure air,
sunshine, gorgeous Colorado mountains.
Great food.*

Great Escapes
Muddle Cottage, Coopers Green,
East Sussex TN22 4AT
t 01825 733422
e jane.dickinson@talk21.com
w www.greatescapes.contactbox.co.uk
*Wonderful weekends in country houses (not
hotels) throughout England. Lacemaking,
beading, embroidery, cross stitch. Beginners,
improvers and advanced. Partners welcome.*

HF Holidays Ltd
Imperial House, Edgware Road, London
NW9 5AL
t 020 8905 9556 **f** 020 8205 0506
e info@hfholidays.co.uk
w www.hfholidays.co.uk
*Holiday courses in country house hotels, on egg
decorating, parchment craft, pattern cutting,
learning to make bobbin lace and calligraphy.*

Hilltop

Windmill Cross, Canterbury Road, Lyminge, Folkestone, Kent CT18 8HD
t 01303 862617
e info@handspin.co.uk
w www.handspin.co.uk
Bespoke textile breaks in rural Kent for individuals or parties of maximum four. See also Mail Order Suppliers (Weaving/Spinning/Feltmaking); Private Colleges and Workshop Organisers; Publications; Textile Tours; Websites; ad on p. 47.

Val Holmes

La Boulinerie, Chevrette, 85370 Nalliers, France
t +33 2 51 30 91 48 **f** +33 2 51 30 93 29
e Boulinerie@aol.com
w www.gitesvendee.com
Embroidery, drawing, design, machine embroidery workshops with author of 'Gardens in Embroidery' and 'The Machine Embroiderer's Workbook'. Activities for non-embroiderers.

Horncastle College

Mareham Road, Horncastle, Lincs LN9 6BW
t 01507 522449 **f** 01507 524382
e horncastle.college@lincolnshire.gov.uk
Offering a variety of short activity breaks including tapestry weaving and dyeing courses on the edge of the Lincolnshire Wolds.

Denise Huddleston

Studio by the Lake, Beacon Cottage, Lake Bank, Water Yeat, via Ulverston, Cumbria LA12 7LS
t 01229 885629
e moonshadowdh@aol.com
Professional tuition, workshops and holidays. Mixed media, contemporary embroidery, jewellery-making and 3-D textile craft in a spectacular setting by the lake.

La Maison du Patchwork

29 rue Jeanne d'Arc, 87290 Chateauponsac, France
t +33 555 76 51 23 **f** +33 555 76 51 23
e maisonpatchwork@aol.com
w hometown.aol.com/maisonpatchwork
Patchwork and quilting residential workshops in beautiful surroundings with internationally known tutors from the UK, Europe and Australia.

Liz Maidment

'Les Romarins', Roman, 30630 Cornillon, France
t +33 4 66 82 38 31
e liz-broderie@wanadoo.fr
w www.lizembroidery.com
5-day workshops in lovely Provence: create a stitched picture with paint, hand/machine embroidery. Beautiful house, pool, good food & wine. Very relaxing! See ad on p. 30.

Metropolitan

The Pinfold, Poole, Nantwich, Cheshire CW5 6AL
t 01270 628414 **f** 01270 610038
e metromachineknit@btconnect.com
w www.metropolitanmachineknitting.co.uk
Mail order - yarns, books, accessories. Machine knitting tuition, residential courses, correspondence courses, video tuition. For all your machine knitting needs.

National Knitting Centre

St Oran's Road, Buncrana, Co Donegal, Ireland
t +353 776 2355 **f** +353 776 2357
e cranaknits@eircom.net
w www.cranaknits.com
Visit our knitting workshop and see the work in progress. Tuition provided for groups.

Normandy Textile Workshop

32 Colville Drive, Bishop's Waltham, Southampton SO32 1LT
t 01489 891225
e anneriches@another.com
w www.normandytextileworkshop.co.uk
Inspirational textile courses taught in the beautiful Normandy countryside. Patchwork, quilting, embroidery, fabric dyeing, etc. One hour from Cherbourg.

Janet Phillips

Warden's House, Bix Bottom, Henley-on-Thames, Oxon RG9 6BL
t 01491 641727
Day workshops and residential courses in woven fabric design, rug weaving, dyeing and spinning. Commission weaving of fabrics.

Sheila Rabbetts Embroidery Breaks

The Cottage, Chapel Lane, Tregrehan Mills,
St Austell, Cornwall PL25 3TH
t 01726 812974
e info@theoldmillcottage.co.uk
w www.theoldmillcottage.co.uk
*Stitch and relax in quiet Cornish village. Near
Eden Project and Heligan. Delightful cottage and
garden. Near woods and streams.*

Dianne Standen

104 High Street, Maryport, Cumbria
CA15 6EQ
t 01900 813378
w www.creative-textiles.co.uk
*Feltmaking/recycling textiles. 2-day workshops.
2-4 participants choose options.
Vegetarian cooking, accommodation in listed
Georgian house overlooking sea/Scotland. See
also Private Colleges and Workshop Organisers;
Textile Artists and Designers; Websites.*

Summer Schools

Dept of Continuing Education, Lancaster University

Lonsdale College, Lancaster LA1 4YN
t 01524 592621/592624 **f** 01524 592448
e Conted@lancaster.ac.uk
w www.lancs.ac.uk/users/conted
*Discover creative collage, découpage and other
textile arts with Lancaster University. Day and
weekend courses as well as summer schools.*

Malvern Hills College

Malvern Hills College, Albert Road North,
Malvern, Worcestershire WR14 2YH
t 01684 565351 **f** 01684 561767
e malvernhills@lineone.net
*Established summer school for adults specialising in
art and craft. Over 50 courses on offer with many
textile related. See also Adult and Further Education.*

Oxford Summer School

c/o Gable End, Hatford, Faringdon,
Oxfordshire SN7 8JF
t 01367 710593 **f** 01367 710593
e richard@thespeeds.freeserve.co.uk
w www.oxfordsummerschool.com
*21-26 July 2003, arts, crafts, music, cookery. 30
different creative workshop courses communicat-
ed with enthusiasm and good humour. 9.30 am -
4.30 pm each day. See ad on p. 91.*

Scottish Embroidery Tutors

56 Falloch Road, Mulngavie G66 7RR
*Embroidery summer schools at St Andrews
University, Fife. June-July annually. Mon-Fri
residential.*

Specialist Breaks and Summer Schools by area

Channel Islands
Creative Stitches

East Anglia
Horncastle College

France
Fabric & Threads Plus
Val Holmes
La Maison du Patchwork
Liz Maidment
Normandy Textile Workshop

Ireland
National Knitting Centre

Midlands
Great Breaks - Acorn Activities
Malvern Hills College (Summer Schools)

North East
Artisan

North West
Denise Huddleston
Lancaster University (Summer Schools)
Metropolitan
Dianne Standen

Northern Ireland
Ardess Craft Centre

Scotland
Scottish Embroidery Tutors (Summer Schools)

South East
Hilltop
Janet Phillips

South West
Pie Chambers - Textiles
Oxford Summer School (Summer Schools)
Sheila Rabbetts Embroidery Breaks

Wales
Creative Days, The Old Vicarage
Pat Gibson
Great Breaks - Acorn Activities

UK
Great Escapes
HF Holidays Ltd

USA
Great Divide Weaving School

Creative journeys - indulging one's passion

How many of us, I wonder, long for the chance to get away from the hubbub of our busy lives in order simply to sit and stitch (or bead, or weave, or whatever is our particular passion) without interruption?

These days there seem to be more and more opportunities to do just that. While collecting information for the relevant sections of *The Textile Directory*, I have been sorely tempted by the stitching holidays offered in France by Liz Maidment, Val Holmes and Gill Thompson (Fabric & Threads Plus) as well as the closer-to-hand weekend courses run by Great Escapes, Missenden Abbey, Dillington House and Westhope College, to name but a few.

Spoilt for choice last winter I packed up my sewing kit and headed for the hills. Or to be more precise, the gorgeous unspoilt countryside of the Welsh borders. I had booked a two-day course with Bobby Britnell at The Old Vicarage, Llansilin,

The Old Vicarage, Llansilin, Oswestry, Shropshire

west of Oswestry in Shropshire. The setting was perfect. The Old Vicarage is a lovely Georgian house set in gardens with fabulous views of the Welsh hillsides. Pam Johnston, the owner, runs Creative Days, Courses in Arts, Crafts and Country Skills in her sunny studio here. She also provides excellent bed and breakfast. My room was very comfortable with a shower room en suite. Arriving after a long drive I was made comfortable with a cup of tea in the guest's sitting room and felt immediately at home.

Supper was served at the local pub where my fellow-guest and I were made very welcome. Llansilin is a tiny but very friendly village, a perfect 'get-away-from-it-all' spot. If you can tear yourself away from your sewing machine I can highly recommend the walking around here. The views are spectacular and the air exhilaratingly fresh.

The course, 'Inspired by Monet', began the next morning, after one of Pam's sumptuous breakfasts. Bobby is an inspiring and extremely lively teacher and the two-day course was surprisingly comprehensive, exploring research and recording of information, elements of design and composition, and evaluating work, as well as

presenting excellent techniques for surface preparation using bondaweb and layers of fabrics. We also looked at xpandaprint, fibre film and foiling methods. Having done all this it was amazing we got to stitch, but we did! Bobby's workshops are packed with useful and thought-provoking information but she still manages to leave the individual with enough room to 'do their own thing', a skill that is much appreciated by her students.

For further information on Creative Days at The Old Vicarage, contact Pam Johnston. See p. 87 for details. For Bobby Britnell see Textile Artists, p. 94.

My next trip was a shorter one, but no less enjoyable. Lying in the very heart of England, The Beetroot Tree, art gallery and workshop studio, must be one of the most conveniently placed textile art venues in the country. Draycott in Derbyshire is 3 miles from junction 25 on the M1, between Nottingham and Derby. It is well worth a visit, but check out their website before you go to see if you can get on one of their excellent day workshops. The Beetroot Tree is run by textile artist, Alysn Midgelow-Marsden. It is housed in a beautifully converted Jacobean barn set in a lovely garden with exhibition spaces inside and out.

On the bookmaking day I went on, Alysn was teaching the craft of Japanese stab-binding. These books are excellent for textile artists because of their concertina-ed spine that leaves lots of room inside for bulky samples, unlike more traditionally bound books. She also teaches maze books and stick books when time permits. Plenty of other courses are available with Alysn or with visiting teachers (Art Van Go were up there for two days last summer). As well as textile art classes, they also run 'Root & Branch' on Saturday mornings; practical sessions for gardeners of all abilities. All day courses include a delicious vegetarian lunch They also sell art materials from Art Van Go. Highly recommended. See ad opposite for contact details.

Sue Richardson, September 2002

Textile Artists and Designers

Acorn/Conceptual Knitted Textiles
35-37 St Marys Gate, Nottingham NG1 1PU
t 0115 958 1114 f 0115 950 4074
e design@acorn-swatches.com
A collection of knitted textile designs created in luxury yarns in innovative concepts including handknitting, crochet and embroidery.

Zainab Ali
8 Horatio Place, 118 Kingston Road, London SW19 1LY
t 07956 455853
e zainab121@hotmail.com
My work is all about form, colour, line and space. I spontaneously paint on silk with acid dyes which is then steamed and pleated. See ad on p. 98.

Alice & Astrid
71 Saltram Crescent, London W9 3JS
t 020 8960 7790 f 020 8960 7284
e astrid@aliceandastrid.com
w www.aliceandastrid.com
Luxury lounge, nightwear and accessories. Wholesaler and manufacturing contacts. Quality, detail and colour are the cornerstone to each collection.

Kay Anderson 🏵
The Studio, 136a Blake Street, Little Aston, Sutton Coldfield, West Midlands B74 4EU
t 0121 352 0059 f 0121 352 0059
e kay-e.anderson@virgin.net
w www.kayanderson.com
Author/fashion designer/lecturer. Sewing courses on capsule wardrobe, waistcoats, stretchknits. Demonstrator for John Lewis stores in Ribbons and Haberdashery.

Nadine Arbuthnot 🏵
48 Drumagarner Road, Kilrea, Coleraine, Co. Londonderry, N Ireland BT51 5TE
t 02829 540224/02890 681665
e nadine.arbuthnot@btopenworld.com
Lecturer/artist specialising in free machine embroidery on water soluble fabric. Commissions undertaken. Tuition to all levels, including City & Guilds.

Artika Designs/Linda Jackson
The Old Rectory, Combpyne, Axminster, Devon EX13 8SY
t 01297 443918 f 01297 445029
e artika@compuserve.com
w www.artika.co.uk
Collections of original abstract charted designs for stitch-based textiles - hand and machine knitting, needlepoint, cross stitch and rugmaking. See also Mail Order Suppliers (General Needlecraft; Knitting/Crochet; Rugmaking).

Bethan Ash - Quilt Artist
3 Hendy Street, Roath Park, Cardiff CF23 5EU
e ash.roath@tesco.net
w www.bethanash.cjb.net
As a quiltmaker, I concentrate on the concept, colour and design of a piece, rather than the traditional technique of assemblage.

Yvonne Autie 🏵
Derwent House, 24 Church Street, North Creake, Fakenham, Norfolk NR21 9AD
t 01328 738131
e yvonne_autie@hotmail.com
Rag rugs: Ilustrated lectures given; commissions; tools; courses, maximum 6 students, beginners welcome, mail order, have fun recycling!

Gilda Baron 🏵
27 Flambard Road, Harrow HA1 2NB
t 020 8907 3950
e baronzeit@aol.com
w www.gildabaron.com
Solo exhibitions, also with groups.Talks, workshops, writes magazine articles, books. 'The Art of Embroidered Flowers', published Autumn 2003.

Lorna Bateman (Vari-Galore) 🏵
5 Bennet Close, Alton, Hants GU34 2EL
t 01420 80595 f 01420 80595
e lorna@varigalore.com
w www.varigalore.com
Workshops and ongoing classes in creative, 3D hand embroidery including crewelwork, ribbonwork, stumpwork, etc. Mail order and open days. See also Mail Order Suppliers (Embroidery).

Diane Bates **t**
132 Sackup Lane, Darton, Barnsley,
South Yorkshire S75 5AR
t 01226 383252
*Day schools. Weekends, summer schools in
machine embroidery and drawing. Lectures on
my ongoing Painted Lady collection.*

Jan Beaney **t**
233 Courthouse Road, Maidenhead,
Berkshire SL6 6HF
t 01628 634503 **f** 01628 675699
w www.doubletrouble-ent.com
*Jan Beaney is an international textile artist,
teacher, lecturer, co-founder of Double Trouble
and member of the 62 Group.*

Melinda Berkowitz **t**
78 Galleywood Road, Great Baddow,
Chelmsford, Essex CM2 8DN
t 01245 475274 **f** 01245 478396
e melinda@galleywood.demon.co.uk
*Textile artist specialising in silk painting,
textured and embellished surfaces. Available for
workshops, lectures, demonstrations. Suitable for
all levels.*

Josiane Bertin-Guest **t**
10 Parkcroft Road, Lee, London SE12 0TA
t 020 8851 4695 **f** 020 8851 4695
e bertin_guest@hotmail.com
w www.embroideryeastwest.co.uk
*Chinese embroidery. Tuition. Design kits
(exclusive). Commission work undertaken.
Creative design and colour workshop and
appraisal of antique oriental textiles.*

Sue Blake
8 Hazely, Tring, Herts HP23 5JH
t 01442 824694
e blake@stitch.demon.co.uk
w www.imagesinstitch.co.uk
*Stitched textiles for sale and commission.
Specialist in machine embroidery, bags and
delicate stitchery for wedding and evening
dresses.*

Jane Blonder - The Eye of the Sun **t**
Beeston Farm, Marhamchurch, Bude,
Cornwall EX23 0ET
t 01288 381 638
e jane@eyeof the sun.com
w www.eyeofthesun.com
*Retreat workshops designed to create a mandala;
a textile wall-hanging based on the principles of
sacred geometry. See also House of Hemp in Mail
Order Suppliers (Knitting/Crochet; Weaving/
Spinning/Feltmaking); ad on p. 47.*

Chris Bojan **t**
20 Heath Drive, Chelmsford, Essex
CM2 9HD
t 01245 256579
e chrisbojan@zoo.co.uk
*C&G's Creative Studies tutor, Embroidery/
Preparing Working Designs. Weekend classes at
North Essex Community College.*

Duncan Booth Design Studio
Windy Bank Lane, Liversedge,
West Yorkshire WF15 8HE
t 01274 861601 **f** 01274 851939
e accounts@duncanboothdesign.com
w www.duncanboothdesign.com
*Independent design studio specialising in design
and colour development for the carpet industry
with trialling service.*

Richard Box **t**
The Red House, Symonds Yat West,
Nr Ross-on-Wye, Herefordshire HR9 6BW
t 01600 890 724
*Richard is an artist working in drawing,
painting and embroidery, a teacher, lecturer
and author.*

Michael Brennand-Wood
130 High Street, Wrestlingworth, Sandy,
Beds SG19 2EJ
t 01767 631380 **f** 01767 631380
*Maker of individual textile and mixed media
work for exhibition and architectural
commission. Exhibited, lectured curated shows
worldwide since 1977.*

Chrissy Bristow ⓣ
1 Highbury Villas, Ash Green Road,
Ash Green, Surrey GU12 6JF
t 01252 312326
e chrissy.bristow@virgin.net
w www.chrissybristow.co.uk
Bead artist and braidmaker (Kumihimo).
Commissions, workshops on off-loom beadwork
and bead crochet for all abilities. See also Beads,
Beads, Beads; Private Colleges and Workshop
Organisers (Creative Needles).

Bobby Britnell ⓣ
Moor Hall Farmhouse, Bettws-y-Crwyn,
Newcastle on Clun, Shropshire SY7 8PH
t 01547 510664
e bobby@bobbybritnell.co.uk
Inspirational design/textile workshops. All ages,
levels and masterclasses. Illustrated lectures.
Welcomes new opportunities to create, exhibit
and sell work.

Janice Britz ⓣ
Studio 1N10, Phoenix Arts Association,
10-14 Waterloo Place, Brighton BN2 2NB
t 07818 417952
e janice@janbritz.com
w www.janbritz.com
Feltmaker, specialising in hats, bags and scarves,
also cobweb felt for interior design uses.
Enthusiastic feltmaking demonstrations, talks
and tuition.

Rachel Brooks ⓣ
11 Gunthorpe Road, Werrington,
Peterborough PE4 7TG
t 01733 571884/07968 287226
e ukiah_uk@hotmail.com
Fashion designer aiming to produce artistic,
unusual, eyecatching fabrics for exclusive,
discerning clientele. Commissions undertaken
for designer outfits or fabrics.

Ann Brown ⓣ
32 Heathlands, Thorrington, Essex CO7 8JR
t 01206 250462
I am first and foremost a C&G Embroidery tutor
(see North Essex Adult Community College)
then a textile artist/designer.

Lee Brown Textile Artist and Tutor ⓣ
4 St James Road, Royal Tunbridge Wells,
Kent TN1 2JZ
t 01892 530927
e postmaster@theoutback.demon.co.uk
C&G Patchwork & Quilting and Embroidery
tutor. Also one-day workshops, summer schools
and freelance lecturer. Commissions undertaken.

Pauline Burbidge
Allanbank Mill, Steading, Allanton, Duns,
Berwickshire TD11 3JX, Scotland
t 01890 818073 **f** 01890 818073
e pb-cp@allanbank.freeserve.co.uk
w www.artstream.com/pburbdet.htm
Collaged, stitched and quilted, large-scale textile
wallhangings. Visit our 'open-studio' exhibition,
held over first weekend of August.

Linda Burden ⓣ
11 New Park Road, Chichester, Sussex
PO19 1XH
t 01243 776969
e lindaburden@hotmail.com
Workshops/courses/commissions by rag rug
designer maker working with wide variety of recy-
cled materials/fabrics exploring colour/texture.

Stephanie Burnham ⓣ
Lavender Cottage, 19 Lower Street,
Pury End, Towcesterl, Northants NN12 7NS
t 01327 811101 **f** 01327 811101
e stephanie@thebeadscene.com
Designer of three-dimensional textile creations in
stumpwork and surface embroidery. Unique
beadwork designs. Available for workshops.

Cilla Cameron Rug Maker ⓣ
The Rug Studio, 18 Elmcroft, Oxton, Notts
NG25 0SB
t 0115 965 5287/07752 772474 **f** 0115 965 5287
e cilla@jpcameron.fsnet.co.uk
w www.nowanowa.com/ragrugs
Rag rug workshops/courses, rug schools,
commissions, supplier of hooks, hessian, frames,
video, books, dyes, wide range of hand-dyed
material.

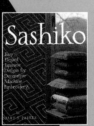

Dawn Cameron-Dick 🅣
1 Manor Barns, Carebey, Stamford,
Lincs PE9 HEA
t 01780 411060 **f** 01780 411060
e ima_dawn@hotmail.com
w morningstarquilts.com
*Travels the UK teaching various patchwork
classes suitable for any ability quilter.
Lighthearted lecture available. Author of
bestselling 'Invisible Machine Appliqué'.*

Val Campbell-Harding 🅣
Long Thatch, Vernham Dean, Andover,
Hampshire SP11 0LE
t 01264 737266 **f** 01264 737266
e val@vch.demon.co.uk
*Courses on machine embroidery, design for
embroidery, beading, passementerie and
computer design.*

Jacqui Carey 🅣
Summercourt, Ridgeway, Ottery St Mary,
Devon EX11 1DT
t 01404 813486 **f** 01404 813486
e carey@careycompany.com
w www.careycompany.com
*Braidmaker (specialist in Kumihimo) for all
requirements and expertise. Commissions,
exhibition work, demonstrations, classes, books,
equipment and threads.*

Annette Claxton Quiltmaker
211 Kings Hall Road, Beckenham, Kent BR3 1LL
t 020 8659 1890
e arthouse@globalnet.co.uk
w www.annette-quilter.com
*Quiltmaker specialising in colour and wallhang-
ings of unique design. Commissions accepted for
quilts of silk, commercial and hand dyed fabrics.*

Karen Clough 🅣
51 Pinewood Drive, Morpeth,
Northumberland NE61 3SS
*I am a tutor, teaching classes in embroidery, silk
painting and feltmaking. I sell work through
local galleries.*

Joy Clucas 🅣
49 Guildford Rd, Colchester, Essex CO1 2RZ
t 01206 868855
*An embroiderer who continues to exhibit as
widely as possible and who will teach or lecture
when invited.*

Lesley Coles Cert. Ed. (FE) 🅣
47 Killyvarder Way, Boscoppa, St Austell,
Cornwall PL25 3DJ
t 01726 61632
e lesley.coles@ntlworld.com
*One-off wall hangings/small quilts. Freelance
writer for specialist magazines. Cards and
patterns available to purchase. See also Adult
and Further Education.*

Jason Collingwood 🅣
31 Gladstone Road, Colchester, Essex CO1 2EA
e jason@rugweaver.co.uk
w www.rugweaver.co.uk
*Workshops and seminars in various techniques of
rugweaving offered. Teaching tours of USA.
Instructional video available. Handwoven rugs to
commission.*

Colwill & Waud
45-46, Charlotte Rd, London EC2A 3PD
t 020 7729 1529 **f** 020 7729 7943
e colwillwaud@aol.com
*Design studio comprising 15 textile designers.
Specialists in home furnishings for print and weave.*

Helen Cowans 🅣
The Crossing, Haugh Head, Wooler,
Northumberland NE71 6QS
t 01668 283193 **f** 01688 283194
e enquiries@purplemoondesigns.co.uk
w www.purplemoondesigns.co.uk
*Designer with a love of silk. Talk and workshop
available. Range of kits and supplies sold through
Purple Moon.*

Kate Cox, Quilt Artist 🅣
82 Brent Terrace, London NW2 1BY
t 020 8458 4119
e katecox@quiltartist.fsnet.co.uk
w www.katecox-quiltartist.co.uk
*I use fabric in a spontaneous, free, impression-
istic way to create my designs. Commissions
taken, lectures and workshops given.*

Louisa & Lewis Creed
27 Norfolk Street, York YO23 1JY
t 01904 624272
e louisacreed@hotmail.com
w www.louisa-creed-ragrugs.co.uk
*Please visit our website, where you will find a
retrospective exhibition of our work plus highly
original ragrug cards.*

Marina Crisp (arriba art) 🔴

Holly House, Crowell Hill, Chinnor, Oxon
OX39 4BT
t 01844 351055
e marina@arribaart.com
w www.arribaart.com
*Marina creates striking silk paintings (using
batik) for your gallery or surroundings,
commissions for industry, textile jewellery and
silk items.*

Michael Crompton - Textile Artist

Forge Cottage, Ireshopeburn, Weardale,
Co Durham DL13 1ER
t 01388 537346
e crompton@tapestryweavers.co.uk
w www.tapestryweavers.co.uk
*International tapestry weaver whose studio and
workshop is open to the public. Tapestries and
wall hangings for sale. Commissions undertaken.*

Nancy Crow 🔴

10545 Snyder Church Rd, Baltimore,
Ohio 43105, USA
t +1 740-862-6554 **f** +1 740-862-6554
e ncrow@netpluscom.com
w www.nancycrow.com
*Nancy Crow, quilt artist, offers workshops,
designs fabrics and leads arts and crafts tours to
Mexico, Guatemala and South Africa.*

Bailey Curtis Workshops (Omega Dyes) 🔴

10 Corsend Road, Hartpury, Glos GL19 3BP
t 01452 700492 **f** 01452 700492
e bailey@omegadyes.co.uk
w www.omegadyes.co.uk
*'Dyeing to Colour' author, Bailey offers dyeing
workshops to all textile workers. Also feltmaking,
silk 'papers' and fibre fusion combinations. See
also Mail Order Suppliers (Dyes/Silk Paints); ad
on p. 39.*

Mary Day 🔴

Oaksey, Aston Road, Chipping Campden,
Gloucestershire GL55 6HR
t 01386 841059 **f** 01386 841059
e marydaysilks@btinternet.com
*City & Guilds and non-vocational silk painting
courses offered with individual tuition for small
groups all year round.*

Helen Deighan 🔴

Roseglen, Crossways Road, Grayshott,
Hindhead, Surrey GU26 6HG
t 01428 605554 **f** 01428 605554
e helendeighan@supanet.com
w www.crosswayspatch.co.uk
*Dyeing and enhancing dyed fabric with machine
embroidery to create quilts and wallhangings.
Author of 'Dyeing in Plastic Bags'.*

Margaret Dennison 🔴

4 Manor Close, Boughton, Newark, Notts
NG22 9JS
t 01623 861166
e mdennisondesign@talkgas.net
*Highly creative, themed, knitted and stitched tex-
tiles. For apparel, home decor and art works.*

Margaret Docherty 🔴

Ruskin Mill Workshops, Old Bristol Road,
Nailsworth, Gloucestershire GL6 0LA
t 01453 833320
*Textile art - contemporary rag rugs and carpet
bags. Also, hand-rolled fleece into felt.
Workshops throughout the year. Open studio.
See ad on p. 91.*

Jane Dorsett 🔴

5 Neyland Path, Cwmbran NP44 4PX
t 01633 868727 / 01495 751518
*Fibre artist specialising in rag-rugs, bags, etc.
Fabric printing/embroidery/batik/silk
papermaking also available.*

Alison Dupernex 🔴

19 Britannia Square, Worcester WR1 3DG
t 01905 726937 **f** 01905 726937
e alison-dupernex@fsmail.net
*Aim - to make a work of art to wear, using
traditional techniques in a contemporary way.
Workshops and presentations available.*

Caroline Earl 🔴

1 Ludwell Cottages, Sunny Hill, Pitcombe,
Somerset BA10 0NN
t 01749 813058 **f** 01749 813058
*Experienced tutor, offers workshops/
demonstrations throughout UK to companies,
private groups and schools. Courses at your
venue, tailored to your needs.*

Falcke & Jones 🅣

Units 5-6 Drumhill Works, Clayton Lane,
Clayton, Bradford, West Yorkshire BD14 6RF
t 01274 880470
e falcke.jones@virgin.net
*Designers specialising in exclusive hand printed
and painted fabrics.*

Pat Gibson 🅣

The Studio, Swn-y-Gwynt, Caersws, Powys
SY17 5HH
t 01686 689048
e pat.gibson@tesco.net
w www.intatexnet.co.uk/lacedesign
*Needlelace specialist. Classes in needlelace,
machine embroidered lace, raised embroidery and
casalguidi at her home or away. Full lists
available. See also Specialist Breaks and Holidays.*

Lynne Gill 🅣

3 Church Cottages, Nursery Lane, North
Wootton, King's Lynn, Norfolk PE30 3QA
t 01553 671178
e flystitch@supanet.com
*I design patchwork, quilting, stitched textiles and
dolls for exhibition and sale; also offer classes and
workshops.*

Valerie Goodbury Silk Paper Workshops 🅣

Willow Cottage, Lower Dingle,
West Malvern, Worcestershire WR14 4BQ
t 01684 563868
*Learn to make a variety of papers from silk fibres,
gossamer fine to 3D! Day courses. Send SAE for
details.*

Martin Green

53 Armson Avenue, Kirby Muxloe, Leicester
LE9 2DB
t 0116 239 3484
*Fine lacy shawls, wraps, stoles, squares and
scarves made on William Lee-type frames
invented in 1589.*

Maggie Grey 🅣

7 Heath Farm Way, Ferndown, Dorset BH22 8JR
t 01202 872429 f 01202 897211
e maggie@workshopontheweb.com
w www.workshopontheweb.com
*Speaker/tutor/writer. Editor of Workshop on the
Web. Recent books 'Layers of Stitch', 'Celtic
Inspirations for Machine Embroiderers' (both
with Val Campbell-Harding). See ad on p. 98.*

Michelle Griffiths @ Rainbow Cottage 🅣

7 Primrose Close, Brackla, Bridgend
CF31 2BS
t 01656 649941 f 01656 649055
e ml.griffiths@virgin.net
w www.rainbowcottage.co.uk
*Embroiderers' Guild Mature Scholar (2001).
Recent work consists of textile art/sculptural
pieces produced using traditional and contemporary shibori techniques.*

Cheryl Hart Textiles 🅣

Studio 5, Pyle Enterprise Centre, Village
Farm, Pyle, Mid Glamorgan CF33 6BL
t 0771 444 3429
e cheryl@cheryl-hart-textiles.com
w www.cheryl-hart-textiles.com
*Designer/manufacturer of quality soft
furnishings/accessories. Antique/modern textiles
embellished with beadwork/hand-dyeing/creative
embroidery. Wholesale haberdashery. Courses
available. See ad on p. 98.*

Jill Hayfield 🅣

Holme Castle, Holmfirth, W Yorkshire
HD9 2QG
t 01484 680680 f 01484 686764
e jill.hayfield@virgin.net
w www.holmecastle.com
*Feltmaking workshops, unique accommodation,
food, residential licence. Studio available for
tutors. Continual exhibitions in gallery. Fibre
sales. Local art tours.*

Christine Heath

Maytree, Mount Pleasant North, Robin
Hood's Bay, Whitby, North Yorks YO22 4RE
t 01947 881045
e cheath@rhbay29.fsnet.co.uk
*Textile artist and paper maker, living in N.
Yorkshire. Hangings and landscape artwork:
mixed media, including feltwork. Commissions
welcomed.*

Sue Hiley Harris 🅣

The Mill, Tregoyd Mill, Three Cocks, Brecon,
Powys LD3 0SW, Wales
t 01497 847421 f 01497 847421
e sue@suehileyharris.co.uk
w www.suehileyharris.co.uk
*Woven sculpture, 3D free-hanging or wall-
mounted relief pieces for domestic settings and
public buildings. Handwoven silk scarves.*

Angie Hughes (t)
Unit 3, Tudor Yard, Lawnside Road,
Ledbury, Herefordshire HR8 2BZ
t 01531 635221
e angiehughes@angiehughes.com
w www.angiehughes.com
*Handprinted and stitched poetry (framed small
pieces, large-scale hangings), courses, talks and
workshops. Handmade cards.*

Sara Impey
Nightingale Cottage, Nightingale Hall Road,
Earls Colne, Colchester, Essex CO6 2NR
t 01787 222937
e impey@tiscali.co.uk
Art quilt designer and maker.

Priscilla Jones BA 'Textile Artist' (t)
16 Leycester Drive, Crosshill, Lancaster LA1
5HW
t 01524 65197
e pi.textiles@ntlworld.com
*A creative and enthusiastic textile artist,
producing textile art for exhibiting, commissions
undertaken, freelance embroidered design and
workshop tuition.*

Helen Keenan (t)
Devon House, 6 Clarence Road, Malvern,
Worcestershire WR14 3DU
t 01684 575835
e helenkeenan@hotmail.com
*This highly original contemporary quilter travels
the creative strandline in fabric, colour and thread.
An experienced and innovative textile teacher.*

Jill Kennedy Textile Artist (t)
3 Cromwell Gardens, Marlow, Bucks SL7 1BG
t 01628 481449 f 01628 481449
e jillkennedy@btinternet.com
w www.jillkennedy.com
*Day workshops and on-line courses in textile
arts - silk painting, batik and surface decoration.
Books, kits and videos available.*

Heather Kingsley-Heath (t)
31 Lower Whitelands, Tyning, Radstock BA3 3JW
t 01761 439262
e heatherworks@btinternet.com
*Textile and beadwork artist, textile sculptures,
beaded installations and jewellery for exhibitions,
private commissions. Writer/journalist on crafts.
Workshop tuition.*

J Kinnersly-Taylor Textile Designer (t)
Studio 005, 77 Hanson Street, Glasgow,
Lanarkshire G31 2HF
t 0141 337 2184 f 0141 337 2184
e joanne.k-t@virgin.net
*Dyed and screen-printed wallhangings and
panels for public, private and gallery spaces.
Range of contemporary table linen.*

Anne Kinniment
Sike View, Kirkwhelpington,
Northumberland NE19 2SA
t 01830 540393
e Anne@kinniment.freeserve.co.uk
w www.kinniment.freeserve.co.uk
*Machine embroidered pictures of rural
Northumberland. Wild flowers and gardens a
speciality.*

Bobbie Kociejowksi (t)
3a Bridge Avenue, Hammersmith, London
W6 9JA
t 020 8748 0924
e bobbiekoc@aladdinscave.net
*Handweaver and teacher. Scarves, shawls and
men's ties in silk, silk and linen, and silk and
wool. Commissions welcomed.*

Ewa Kuniczak (t)
23 Glebe Road, Kincardine-on-Forth, Alloa,
Clackmannanshire FK10 4QB
Scotland
t 01259 730779 f 01259 730779
e ewa@feltheadtotoe.co.uk
w www.feltheadtotoe.co.uk
*Specialising in custom-made fine quality
handmade seamless felt items for adults, children,
the home. Hats, garments, bags, teacosies,
cafetiere covers.*

Ruth Kathryn Lamont BA Hons (Rootie Tootie Designs)
291 Eldon St, Greenock, Renfrewshire
PA16 7QL
t 01475 659315
e rklamont22@yahoo.co.uk
*Printed textile designer. Original creative
designs for all surfaces specialising in industrial
corporate installations and soft furnishings. See
also Conferences/Major Events/Shows.*

Sarah Lawrence
104 Middleton Road, Newark NG24 2DN
t 01636 659890 **f** 01636 706948
e sarah@sarah-lawrence.com
w sarah-lawrence.com
Freelance textile artist specialising in felt,
machine embroidery and beadworks.
Commissions undertaken. Tuition to all levels.

Heidi Lichterman
The Old Courthouse, High Street, Bottisham,
Cambs CB5 9BA
t 01223 811461
e heidi@aleph1.co.uk
I weave large, abstract wall hangings in silk and
wire that are site specific, particularly for
corporate and public spaces.

Hillu Liebelt
15 Shepherds Hill, London N6 5QJ
t 020 8340 7785 **f** 020 8340 7785
Woven tapestries and textile sculptures.

Jean Littlejohn
25 The Crescent, Maidenhead, Berks SL6 6AA
t 01628 630985 **f** 01628 630985
w www.doubletrouble-ent.com
Jean Littlejohn is an international textile artist,
teacher and lecturer and co-founder of Double
Trouble.

Jeff Lowe Papermaking Workshops
5 Avenue Approach, Chichester, West Sussex
PO19 3BQ
t 01243 528046
Courses focus on paper pulps and fibres to create
pieces of textile artform and delightful papers
using innovative techniques.

Lucy Ann Designs
Studio 701-2, The Big Peg, 120 Vyse Street,
Hockley, Birmingham B18 6NF
t 0121 687 7767 **f** 0121 687 7767
e lucyanndesigns@aol.com
Embroidered textiles for bridal and evening wear.
Accessories and dress decoration.

Jennie McCall
281 Beacon Road,Loughborough,
Leicestershire LE11 2RA
t 01509 267507 **f** 01509 214935
e jmctart@aol.com
Multi-media artist specialising in handstitch on
silk paper, Jennie also creates limited editions of
small wire figurines. Commissions undertaken.

Lyn McDermott
Kerian, 13 Norfolk Road, Desford, Leicester
t 01455 823870
e lyn@kerian.freeserve.co.uk
This artist/teacher works with hand and machine
stitch to create contemporary pieces with the
timeless quality of medieval art.

Lis Mann
1 Raincliffe Close, Aynho, Banbury,
Northants OX17 3SB
t 01869 810264
e lismann@supanet.com
Stitched and painted textiles for sale and
commission. Embroidery and mixed media
courses taught in small groups in country
setting. See ad on p. 58.

Julie Marchington
31 Colinton Road, Edinburgh EH10 5DR
t 0131 447 3627 **f** 0131 240 0969
e julie.marchington@hot-toast.com
w www.handknit.co.uk
Original handknitted garments using traditional
stitches in contemporary designs. Knit kits
available.

Barley Massey
Fabrications, 7 Broadway Market, Hackney,
London E8 4PH
Contemporary textile pieces for all kinds of
interiors. Innovative, fun, modern and recycled.
Batch produced, one-offs and commissions.

Sandra Meech
Edgewater, Nash Park, Binfield, Berkshire
RG42 4EN
t 01344 455726
e texarts@aol.com
A stitched textile and quilt artist exhibiting/
teaching in UK/Canada. Workshops for all levels
in colour, design and surface techniques.

Left, woven textiles by Wallace & Sewell at C2+Gallery, see Art Galleries, p. 14.

Below, a selection of knitwear by Alison Dupernex, Textile Artists, p. 97.

Above, 'Celestial Garden', detail of jacket by Theresa Searle, Textile Artists, p. 104.

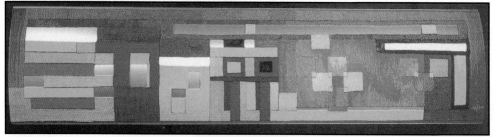

Above, 'Im Spaetrot', 2001, Hillu Liebelt, Textile Artists, p. 101.

many thanks to all of you who sent in pictures of your work and apologies to those we did not have space for

please try again next year

Left, handwoven silk & wool shawl, Bobbie Kociejowski, Textile Artists, p. 100.

Alicia Merrett
43 Anson Road, London N7 OAR
t 020 7609 1013 **f** 020 7609 8648
e alicia@tufpark.demon.co.uk
w www.tufpark.demon.co.uk
Contemporary art quilts: deep colours, abstract shapes, freeform cut and pieced, fused appliquéd. Workshops and courses, lectures, commissions.

Alysn Midgelow-Marsden
The Beetroot Tree, South Street, Draycott, Derbyshire DE72 3PP
t 01332 873929 **f** 01332 873929
e alysn@thebeetroottree.com
w www.thebeetroottree.com
Texture: colour: design: fun: energetic: embroidered and mixed media textiles. Commissions: exhibitions: home and away workshops. For full details contact Alysn. See Beetroot Tree ad on p. 91.

Linda Miller
30 Trinity Close, Stefen Hill, Daventry, Northamptonshire NN11 4RN
t 01327 301972
Fine art textile artist offers workshops and private tuition in rag rugging and contemporary textiles. Commissions also undertaken.

Stuart Morris
The Rose Chapel, George Street, Hadleigh, Ipswich, Suffolk IP7 5BT
t 01473 824212 **f** 01473 824133
e stuart@stuartmorris.co.uk
Working from a converted chapel, Stuart produces large scale printed canvases. These combine texture, pattern and imagery in evocative colours.

Morwen
Cefn Hedog, Pwllheli, Gwynedd LL53 8HL
Designing giftwrap, cards/stationery, childrenswear and general artwork. Any novelty design for textiles.

Sue Munday
Brambles, 32 Blackberry Lane, Selsey, West Sussex PO20 9JW
t 01243 605450
e s.munday@ukonline.co.uk
Experienced tutor and textile artist working in manipulated techniques, using both hand and machine embroidery. List available for talks/workshops.

Rosemary Muntus
Old Mill House, The Causeway, Hitcham, Suffolk IP7 7NF
t 01449 741747 **f** 01449 740118
e rmuntus@aol.com
w www.muntus.co.uk/rosemary
Design, quilting and historical costume consultancy, talks and workshops. Special subjects include computer images, sashiko quilting and Tudor period clothes.

Denise Musk
42 Fernbank Drive, Baildon, Shipley, West Yorkshire BD17 5HY
t 01274 587068
e d.musk@tiscali.co.uk
Fabrics and garments combining machine knitting and machine embroidery. Lectures/workshops - Decorative techniques using mixed media - Design development.

Carol Naylor
2 Jubilee Road, Chichester, West Sussex PO19 7XB
t 01243 782075
e carol.naylor@btopenworld.com
w www.carolnaylor.co.uk
I make machine embroidered textile wall hangings and framed works for interiors for both public and private venues.

Robin Paris
4 The Row, Five Lanes, Launceston, Cornwall PL15 7RX
t 01566 86465
e robin@robinparis.co.uk
w www.robinparis.co.uk
Batik paintings - wildlife, marine, environmental and abstract art using traditional, exploratory and unconventional techniques. Commissions and visitors welcome.

Susan Pearson
58 Butt Lane, Laceby, Grimsby, Lincs DN37 7AH
t 01472 590521
e susan.e.pearson@ntlworld.com
Exhibiting artist also runs workdays in 3D felt, felt for embroidery, braids and tassels, machine embroidered jewellery. Talks and demonstrations.

Yvonne Pedretti

17 Fairways, Wyatts Drive, Thorpe Bay,
Essex SS1 3DB
t 01702 586343
e yvonnepedretti@southend-adult.co.uk
*Wall hangings and sculptural forms in knit and
resin, printed textile (devoré) and machine lace.*

Ragged Fortitude

The Bookshop at The Tinners Rabbit, 48
Market Street, Ulverston, Cumbria LA12 7LS
*Design and make traditional rag rugs to sell and
for commission.*

Jennie Rayment

5 Queen Street, Emsworth, Hampshire
PO10 7BJ
t 01243 374860 **f** 01243 374860
e jenrayment@aol.com
*International lecturer/tutor/author. Uniquely
innovative techniques on rolling, folding,
twiddling, fiddling, stuffing and tucking for
surface texture/fabric manipulation.*

Emma Reynolds

14a Constitution Hill, Ipswich IP1 3RH
t 01473 221011
e emmareynolds14a@hotmail.com
*Both the inspiration and materials for my work
are obtained from insects. Silk, shellac, cochineal
and beeswax. Insect architecture my form.*

Juliet Robson

Unit 9, Kiln Workshops, Pilcot Road,
Crookham Village, Fleet, Hants GU51 5RY
t 01252 622272
e juliet@julietrobson.com
*Painted designs for fabrics, homewares,
stationery, fine art, china and surface patterns.*

Jane Rowe

Shorelines, 2 River Street, Portscatho, Truro,
Cornwall TR2 5HQ
t 01872 580872 **f** 01872 580226
e jerowescatho@macunlimited.net
*Freelance tutor, authority on stumpwork.
Courses on stumpwork, needlelace, hand-
embroidered textiles. 'Stumpwork Techniques -
The Workbook', published 2001.*

Louise Ruth Designs

c/o Walford Mill Craft Centre, Stone Lane,
Wimborne, Dorset BH21 1NL
t 01202 841400 **f** 01202 840132
e louise@louiseruthdesigns.com
w www.louiseruthdesigns.com
*Unique, high-quality cards, gifts and wedding
stationery, hand-created using fabrics and
freehand machine embroidery.*

Joanie San Chirico

1064 Lake Placid Dr, Toms River, NJ 08753,
USA
*Art quilts using textile paint, embroidery and
hand work to create texture in work based on
archaeological themes.*

Teresa Searle

61 Britannia Road, Easton, Bristol BS5 6BZ
t 0117 9350345 **f** 0117 9350345
e teresa.searle@lineone.net
w www.teresasearle.co.uk
*Richly coloured clothing and accessories using
felted knitting with appliqué and embroidery.
Please contact for details of presentations,
workshops and stockists.*

Shades of Heather Workshops

Garden Studio, Greencroft, Reeth,
Richmond, North Yorks DL11 6QT
t 01748 884435
e rugmaker@clara.net
w www.rugmaker.co.uk
*Rug-making workshops. Suppliers of hooks,
prodders, various sizes, evenweave hessian,
stretcher frames, lap frames, books, wool dyes.
Video.*

Lauren Shanley

4 Gabriels Wharf, 56 Upper Ground, London
SE1 9PP
t 020 7928 5782
e laurenshanley@zoom.co.uk
*Hand and machine embroidered clothing, accessories
and interior pieces, made from vintage fabrics.*

Silk Gallery

The Stables, Nannerch, Mold CH7 5RD
t 01352 741893
e bev@silkgallery.org.uk
w www.silkgallery.org.uk
Specialist in silk painting. Original paintings, wall hangings and limited edition prints. Children's and adult workshops. SAE for information. See also Mail Order Suppliers (Dyes/Silk Paints).

Ann Small

Highfields Park Green, Berden, Bishop's Stortford, Herts CM23 1BA
t 01279 777268
e ann@asmalldesign.co.uk
w www.asmalldesign.co.uk
Creating textiles with attitude.

Chrissy Smith

11 Chichester Road, Seaford, Sussex BN25 2DJ
t 01323 490993
Offers workshops in rug-making techniques and machine embroidery skills at various venues or at her home (minimum four people).

Sheila Smith

17 Cleveland Way, Carlton Miniott, Thirsk, North Yorks YO7 4LN
t 01845 523340 f 01845 523340
e sheils@miniott.demon.co.uk
w www.feltbydesign.co.uk
Illustrated talks and practical workshops in all aspects of feltmaking arranged for groups and guilds.

Solstice Moon

'Brooklands', Trebehor, St. Levan, Penzance, Cornwall TR19 6LX
e chris@solsticemoon.fsbusiness.co.uk
w www.solsticemoon.co.uk
Christine Parish is a fashion/textile designer specialising in hand-dyed and devoré or discharged screen-printed limited edition scarves.

Rebecca Spragge

520 Earlham Road, Norwich NR4 7HR
t 01603 502172
e rebeccaspragge@yahoo.co.uk
w www.rebeccaspragge.co.uk
Theatrical designer of wearable art corsets, contemporary, bridal and costume. Has demonstrated at the Victoria & Albert Museum. Tuition available.

Munni Srivastava

80 Trinity Court, Gray's Inn Road, London WC1X 8JY
t 020 7833 2779 f 020 7580 6330
e arttextiles@munnisrivastava.com
w www.munnisrivastava.com
I produce one-off contemporary embroidered wallhangings for private or corporate clients. Exhibit regularly UK and abroad. Commissions welcome. Occasional workshops.

Dianne Standen

104 High Street, Maryport, Cumbria CA15 6EQ
t 01900 813378
w www.creative-textiles.co.uk
I incorporate fascination for texture/colour with environmental concerns to produce felted/hooked rugs, bags, clothes, hangings from waste textiles. See also Private Colleges and Workshop Organisers; Specialist Breaks and Holidays; Websites.

Linda Straw

The Tower House, Rushes Lane, Lubenham, Market Harborough LE16 9TN
t 01858 461988
e linda@linda-straw-quilts.co.uk
w www.linda-straw-quilts.co.uk
A unique method, combining appliqué, embroidery and quilting to produce a rich pictorial textile.

Maggie Swain

49 Shawhurst Lane, Hollywood, Birmingham B47 5HL
t 01564 823944
e maggie.swain1@btopenworld.com
Workshops on machine embroidery incorporating mixed media techniques. A contemporary approach to textile art.

Dionne Swift

c/o JLB, Quay Street, Huddersfield, West Yorkshire HD1 6QT
t 01484 312041 f 01484 312041
e info@dionneswift.co.uk
w www.dionneswift.co.uk
Individually created devoré velvet textiles: hangings, scarves, pictures and books. 2-day devoré workshops and devoré kits by mail order. See ad on p. 98.

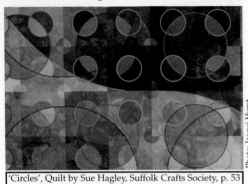

'Circles', Quilt by Sue Hagley, Suffolk Crafts Society, p. 53

Photo: Jacqui Hurst

Taipéis Gael Teo **t**
Malinbeg, Glencolmcille, Co. Donegal, Ireland
t +353 73 30325/30372 **f** +353 73 30325
e taipeisgael@eircom.net
w www.tapeisgael.ie
Tapeis Gael tapestry artists weave unique art tapestries of various sizes for exhibition and to commission.

Margaret Talbot **t**
58 Orchard Way, Cambourne, Cambridge CB3 6BN
e margaret@elmswell.force9.co.uk
Artist using machine embroidery and mixed media to produce wallhangings with a time-worn and medieval appearance. Teaches contemporary embroidery.

Elza Tantcheva **t**
The Limes, Tickenham Hill, Tickenham, Clevedon, North Somerset BS21 6SW
e 01275 857845 **f** 01275 856094
e etan711@aol.com
Hand-woven and hand-felted art and ecclesiastical textiles, fashion accessories and soft furnishing. Main inspiration comes from Byzantine tradition. See also Private Colleges and Workshop Organisers.

Virginia Teague, Handweaver **t**
Chwaen Ddu, Carmel, Llanerchymedd, Anglesey LL71 7DE, North Wales
t 01248 470371 **f** 01248 470371
e virginia@handweaving.co.uk
w www.handweaving.co.uk
Handwoven wraparound shawls etc. in silks and wools. Fabric by the metre. Heritage items researched and reproduced. Commissions welcome. Tuition available.

Joanne Temple
110 Andover Avenue, Alkrington, Middleton, Manchester M24 1JW
t 0161 654 8365
Subtle colours, a range of stitchery and juxtaposition of felt construction carefully brought together creating a range of luxury textiles.

Kim Thittichai Textile Artist and Tutor **t**
126 Norwich Drive, Brighton BN2 4LL
t 01273 694449
Specialising in experimental textiles and surface decoration. Workshops, summer schools and freelance lecturer.

Pat Trott - Beadwork Tutor **t**
82 Halstead Walk, Allington, Maidstone, Kent ME16 0PW
t 01622 750910
Wide range of classes in traditional techniques - needlelace, stumpwork, drawn thread, pulled, assisi, mountmellick, shisha, cutwork, shadow, crewel, hardanger, etc. See also Beads, Beads, Beads.

Cherrilyn Tyler **t**
76 Garland, Rothley, Leicester LE7 7RG
t 0116 237 4686 **f** 0116 237 5346
e directory@cherrilyn.com
w www.cherrilyn.com
Ethereal transparent textile hangings and wearable art. Lectures and workshops throughout the UK. City & Guilds Parts 1, 2 & 3 in Leicestershire.

'Lotus', Chris Bojan, see p. 93.

Melanie Venes (t)
Greenwoods, High Street, Thornham,
Hunstanton PE36 6LY
t 01485 512315
e melanie@twill-knot.freeserve.co.uk
*Design and weave in Norfolk. Handweaver and
teacher offering courses combining design
inspiration with technical advice and tuition.*

Pauline Verrinder (t)
45 Station Road, Willingham, Cambridge
CB4 5HF
t 01954 260358
e pollyverr@aol.com
*Textile artist/tutor working in embroidery and
mixed media techniques.*

Sandra Wallace (t)
3 Ivy Bank, Yeadon, Nr Leeds LS19 7HJ
t 0113 250 7396
e swallacebeadwork@aol.com
*C&G Creative Studies lecturer. Workshops, lec-
tures on beadweaving, embroidery and combined
techniques. Special interest in Native American
beadwork. See also Beads, Beads, Beads.*

(The) Wee Gift Shop (t)
10 Aitken Street, Largs KA30 8AU
t 01475 674102 **f** 01475 675917
e weegiftshop@thefreeinternet.co.uk
*Retail space/studio. See artist at work. Purchase
unique silk accessories. Meet speaker/textile tutor
(Sally Webster) - happy to travel.*

Wern Mill Gallery & Textile Craft (t)
Workshops
Melin-y-Wern, Denbigh Road, Nannerch,
Mold, Flintshire CH7 5RH, Wales
t 01352 741318 **f** 01352 741318
e chrisatwernmill@tiscali.co.uk
w www.wernmillcreative.co.uk
*Professional tuition in restored watermill.
Machine embroidery, painting, printing, batik.
Commissions. Resident artist Christine Garwood
BA (Hons) Textiles (Goldsmiths). See also Mail
Order Suppliers (Embroidery).*

West Dean Tapestry Weavers (t)
Chichester, West Sussex PO18 0QZ
t 01243 811301 **f** 01243 811343
e enquiries@westdean.org.uk
w www.westdean.org.uk
*Award-winning designer-weavers work to
commission for private and corporate clients,
including Historic Scotland, Portcullis House
and Mercers' Company. See also Adult and
Further Education; Higher Education/Research
Centres; Private Colleges and Workshop
Organisers.*

Linda Westerman (t)
5 Meadow Vale, Scawby, Brigg, Lincs
DN20 9EW
t 01652 654816
e tactile.images@uk.gateway.net
*Exhibiting and teaching nationally, Linda blends
hand and machine embroidery and metal threads
on a base of wool fibres and muslin.*

Isabella Whitworth (t)
4 Kingfisher Close, Abingdon, Oxon OX14 5NP
t 01235 527636
e whitworth.silk@virgin.net
w www.isabellawhitworth.co.uk
*Isabella produces resist-dyed scarves and fabrics.
Best known for silk-painting, she offers courses in
this and related techniques. See ad on p. 91.*

Rosemary Wilkes (t)
Preston Mill Cottage, Preston Road,
East Linton EH40 3DS
t 01620 860334
Tuition in handspinning and natural dyeing.

David Yarrington Studios Ltd (t)
112 Bolling Rd, Ilkley, West Yorkshire
LS29 8PN
t 01943 605605 **f** 01943 605606
e david.yarrington@btinternet.com
w davidyarringtonstudios.com
*Design and colour consultants to the
floorcovering industry internationally.*

Textile Tours

Andrew Brock Travel
29a Main Street, Lyddington, Oakham,
Rutland LE15 9LR
t 01572 821330 f 01572 821072
e abrock3650@aol.com
w www.andrewbrocktravel.co.uk
*Expert-led small group tours to study textiles
and handicrafts in India and elsewhere.*

Art Workshops in Guatemala 🅣
4758 Lyndale Avenue South, Minneapolis,
MN 55409-2304, USA
t +1 612 825 0747 f +1 612 825 6637
e info@artguat.org
w www.artguat.org
*10-day educational travel programmes in a wide
variety of arts, e.g. loom beading, backstrap
weaving, papermaking/book art, silk painting.*

British-Bulgarian Friendship Society 🅣
Balkania Travel, 28 Hawgood Street,
London E3 3RU
t 020 7237 7616 f 020 7237 7616
e drannie.kay@aol.com
w www.bbfs.org.uk
*Bulgaria: escorted spring tour. Ethnographic
museums (some reserve collections), master
classes and demonstrations. Picturesque scenery.
Two weeks for £900.*

FLEWS 🅣
PO Box 121, Reigate RH2 9YU
t 01737 245464/01273 473552
e nyasa@globalnet.co.uk
w www.flews.co.uk
*Global textile retreat 6-13 July, Czorsztyn,
Pieniny Mountains, southern Poland.
Feltmaking, bobbin lacemaking, embroidery,
paper arts. International tutors.*

Hilltop 🅣
Windmill Cross, Canterbury Road, Lyminge,
Folkstone, Kent CT18 8HD
t 01303 862617
e info@handspin.co.uk
w www.handspin.co.uk
*Bespoke textile tours in rural Kent for individuals
or parties of maximum four. See also Mail Order
Suppliers (Weaving/Spinning/Felt); Private
Colleges/Workshop Organisers; Publications;
Specialist Breaks; Websites; ad on p. 47.*

Icelandic Tapestry School & Jona 🅣 Tours
Southleigh, Langport Road, Somerton,
Somerset TA11 6RT
t 01458 273111 f 01458 273111
e jonasparey@n-iceland.com
w www.n-iceland.com
*Mainly Iceland but tours to other countries
incorporating visits to textile museums and
private collections. Plus courses and lectures.*

India Link 🅣
16 Catherine Hill, Frome, Somerset BA11 1B2
t 01373 455690 f 01373 455992
w www.indialinktravel.co.uk
*Specialised escorted journeys in India with a
focus on art, crafts and textiles. Many practical
workshops included.*

Indian Romance
46 Masbro Road, London W14 0LT
t 020 7603 9616 f 020 7371 1917
e lorna@indianromance.demon.co.uk
w www.indianromance.co.uk
*Textiles, painting and arts cultural tours to
India. Experiencing India through the focus of
textiles or painting is greatly enriching.*

JJN Amish Quilts 🅣
45 Kathie Road, Bedford MK42 0QJ
t 01234 356785 f 01234 356785
e ycv70@dial.pipex.com
w www.amishquilts.co.uk
*Jan Jefferson offers tours to Lancaster County,
Pennsylvania, as well as lectures, workshops,
studydays about the Amish and their quilts.*

Les Arts Vivants 🅣
Chateau Monferrier, 24330 St Pierre de
Chignac, France
t +33 55 30 67 536 f +33 55 30 60 882
e lesartsvivants@aol.com
w www.lesartsvivants.com
*Residential courses in textile history and
decorative arts with visits to collections at
museums and chateaux. Pool, tennis, great food.*

Websites

about.com
w home.about.com/hobbies/index.htm
Interest groups, patterns, tips, online classes and chat on beadwork, crochet, cross stitch, knitting, needlepoint, quilting and sewing.

(The) African Fabric Shop
w www.africanfabrics.co.uk
Fabrics to order. Quilt Gallery. Workshops & Talks.

Aion
w www.aion-needlecrafts.co.uk
Designs, cross stitch penpals, list of UK needlecraft sites and resource library.

Art Sketch Book
w www.artsketchbook.com
A free site to search for, display and email art.

British Quilt Study Group
w www.quiltstudy.org.uk
Formed in 1998 by the Quilters' Guild of the British Isles to promote appreciation, knowledge and understanding of the heritage of patchwork and quilting.

Celia Eddy's Quilt Story
w www.quilt.co.uk
A well-designed site featuring articles, book reviews, events, penpal board, message board, 'what's on' and classified ads.

Cross Stitch Club
w www.cross-stitch-club.com
Meet, make friends, share experiences and ideas.

(The) Embroidery Exchange
46 Barton Court Road, New Milton,
Hampshire BH25 6NR
t 01425 617650
e befriend@theembroideryexchange.com
w www.theembroideryexchange.com
Buy, sell or exchange equipment for stitched textiles on the website, study stitched textiles and fabric decoration in the studio. See ad on p. 91.

FibreArtsOnline
w www.fibreartsonline.com
An internet connection to the fibrearts community. Provides links to the websites where information is available for fibre artists.

Maggie Grey's Workshop on the Web
7 Heath Farm Way, Ferndown, Dorset BH22 8JR
t 01202 872429 f 01202 897211
e maggie@workshopontheweb.com
w www.workshopontheweb.com
Fancy a workshop with a top tutor such as Val Campbell-Harding, Ruth Issett or Maggie Grey? Online embroidery classes. See ad on p. 98.

Hilltop
Windmill Cross, Canterbury Road, Lyminge,
Folkestone, Kent CT18 8HD
t 01303 862617
e info@handspin.co.uk
w www.handspin.co.uk
Small or medium-size bespoke website design and upload to own or supplied website. See also Mail Order Suppliers (Weaving/Spinning/Felt); Private Colleges/Workshop Organisers; Publications; Specialist Breaks; Textile Tours; ad on p. 47.

India Crafts
w www.india-crafts.com
Explore the history of Indian textiles; also printing, appliqué and many more techniques.

(The) Internet Craft Fair
w www.craft-fair.co.uk
A cornucopia of crafts in the UK, with details of crafters, suppliers, craft guilds, organisations and forthcoming craft events.

(The) Needlecraft Fair
w www.needlecraft-fair.co.uk
For UK suppliers, guilds, events and magazines for embroidery, cross stitch, knitting, crochet, sewing, needlepoint, quilting, patchwork, lacemaking and other needlecrafts.

Online Fabrics
388-394, Foleshill Rd, Coventry CV6 5AN
t 024 7668 7776
w www.online-fabrics.co.uk
The leading fabric retailer on the web today. Huge range of fabrics delivered straight to your doorstep. Free membership.

Rowan and Jaeger Handknits

Green Lane Mill, Holmfirth, W Yorks
HD9 2DX
t 01484 681881 **f** 01484 687920
e mail@knitrowan.com
w www.knitrowan.com
The best in handknitting design with a range of knitting magazines, beautiful yarns and knitting courses nationwide. See also Adult and Further Education; Mail Order Suppliers (Knitting/Crochet); Publications.

(The) Small Website Company

3 Bellerophon Drive, Penicuik, Edinburgh
EH26 8NU
e small@3bellerophon.freeserve.co.uk
Showcase your work on an affordable website developed specifically for artists and designers. Go to 'www.asmalldesign.co.uk' for an example.

Solusheet

w www.husqvarnastudio.co.uk
Water-dissolvable fabric suitable for embroidery and many other sewing applications.

Splut

w www.splut.com
Banner-free directory of UK websites. Includes a small section on Textiles in Arts & Humanities/Crafts.

Dianne Standen

104 High Street, Maryport, Cumbria
CA15 6EQ
t 01900 813378
w www.creative-textiles.co.uk
Lots of examples of experimental work in gallery section. Details of courses. Mail order felt slippers. See also Private Colleges and Workshop Organisers; Specialist Breaks and Holidays; Textile Artists and Designers.

TFL Fabrics

w www.tflfabrics.com
Online fabric shop specialising in fabrics sourced from around the world.

Temari

w www.temari.com
The art of Japanese threadballs. History, books, and how-to's on a thousand-year-old craft from Japan.

Textile Fairs (Artfairs)

w www.artizania.co.uk
Artizania - wide range of antique/vintage costume/textiles offered for sale. Artfairs - details of specialist antique costume & textiles fairs.

Textile Source

w www.textilesource.com
Database for textile companies. Also textile design, journals and magazines. Seminars and library of recommended books.

(The) Thread Studio

6 Smith Street, Perth 6000, Western Australia
t +61 8 9227 1561 **f** +61 8 9227 0254
e mail@thethreadstudio.com
w www.thethreadstudio.com
Speciality embroidery threads and textile art supplies by mail order. Our shop is in cyberspace. Also 'Playways on the Net' textile art course.

Tough Treasures

w www.toughtreasures.freeuk.com
Hand-dyed threads and fabrics for your imagination.

www.fabrics4you.co.uk

30 Capehill, Smethwick, Birmingham
B66 4PB
t 0121 555 5047 **f** 0121 246 1254
e fabrics@fabrics4you.co.uk
w www.fabrics4you.co.uk
Online fabric store.

www.kidsfabrics.co.uk

Dryslwyn House, 25, Llandeilo Road,
Brynamman, Ammanford, Dyfed SA18 1BA
t 01269 825796 **f** 01269 826972
e sales@kidsfabrics.co.uk
w www.kidsfabrics.co.uk
Furnishing fabric retailer for childrens' rooms. Fabrics viewed online. Sample and free design service via email, fax or phone.

Wonderful Stitches WWW

w www.needlework.com
Resources for stitchery enthusiasts.

Wool Works - The Online Knitting Compendium

w www.woolworks.org
Non-commercial, volunteer-run site full of information for handknitters.

Index

This index lists the names of the individuals, companies and organisations with entries in *The Textile Directory 2003*. To help you find that half-remembered name, we have listed them in as many ways as possible – for example, you will find people listed in the format "Firstname Lastname" as well as in the conventional inverted indexing format of "Lastname, Firstname". Definite and indefinite articles (a, an, the) at the beginning of names are always inverted. Page numbers in *italics* indicate advertisements. Page numbers in **bold** indicate an editorial mention, for example in an article or the caption to a photograph.

listings by geographical area appear at the end of relevant sections

the contents list for mail order suppliers is on p. 31

117